SALISBURY

THE CHANGING CITY

The view up St Ann Street, as depicted in Hall's ***Picturesque Memorials***, 1834. At the extreme left is Moorland House, demolished in 1964. No.82, next door, is now the St Ann Street surgery.

SALISBURY
THE CHANGING CITY

BRUCE PURVIS

Published in association with

First published in Great Britain byThe Breedon Books Publishing Company Limited
Breedon House, 44 Friar Gate, Derby, DE1 1DA. 1999

This paperback edition published in Great Britain in 2015 by DB Publishing, an imprint of
JMD Media Ltd

ISBN 978-1-78091-504-3

Printed and bound in Great Britain by Marston Book Services Ltd, Oxfordshire

CONTENTS

Dedication

To my parents Bob and Diana Purvis
on the occasion of their diamond
wedding anniversary.

ACKNOWLEDGEMENTS

ADDING to the bibliography of a city whose history is as well-rehearsed as Salisbury's involves facing quite distinctive challenges. In particular, I am conscious of inheriting, and trying to build upon, the work of historians from the past quarter of a millennium; in the recent past, that of John Chandler. Without knowledge of his work, my own efforts would have had to have been immeasurably greater, and the likely outcome correspondingly impoverished. At a personal level I owe an enormous debt of gratitude to my publishers, and especially my commissioning editor, Rupert Harding, for his enthusiasm for my idea, his continuing encouragement and his belief in the project throughout its gestation.

My thanks go to my colleagues at Salisbury Library and Galleries, and my wife and family for their forbearance over the many months during which I have faced the world with a somewhat distracted air during the preparation of this book. Peter Saunders, Director of the Salisbury and South Wiltshire Museum, and his staff have been unfailingly kind in their help in locating artefacts and images from their wealth of resources for inclusion in the book. Jane Standen, in particular, has been unstintingly generous with her time and attention. Tim Tatton-Brown read an early draft of Chapter 3, and I have benefited enormously from his detailed comments and suggestions, and, for other concerns, from his introductions to Richard Gem and John Carley.

For permission to use images which are their property and/or their copyright I wish to thank the Trustees and Director of the Salisbury and South Wiltshire Museum, Alun Williams, Visitor Services Manager, for permission on behalf of the dean and chapter of Salisbury Cathedral to undertake photography of the cathedral and for an illustration of the Salisbury Magna Carta, Caroline Johanneson, Publicity Manager at Salisbury District Council, for permission on the Council's behalf for images from the Lovibond Collection and from Thomas Sharp's 1949 Report to the City Council, the Editor of the ***Salisbury Journal*** for illustrations from the ***Salisbury Times***, Wiltshire County Council for images from its archival, print and photographic collections and the Salisbury Millennium Photograph and the Trustees of the Edwin Young Collection for some of Young's watercolours.

On more specific matters, I wish to record my gratitude to: Diana Crichton for alerting me to the ***Ballad of Colonel Penruddock***, David Brown for access to the images of Bloom's shop and the breviary according to the Use of Sarum, Richard Gem on the layout of the cathedral at Old Sarum, John Carley for access to the Close Ditch, Ron Todd for information on the coinage minted at Old Sarum, Jad Bienek, Bill Chorley, Peter Goodhugh, Jane Howells, Mike Marshman, Ruth Newman and Eve Shillingford for their encouragement and interest generally, Pam Robinson for her navigational skills among the ephemera collection in Salisbury Library, Les Mitchell, for information on the Gibbs, Mew premises in Gigant Street, Vince Jenkins for drawing my attention to the alignment of the Harnham Gate and its significance for the chronology of the Close, Sue Johnson for drawing my attention to the Milford Street streetscape, Helen Philp for drawing my attention to a poem in the ***Salisbury Journal***, Barbara, my wife, for guiding me to Pontigny, the last resting-place of St Edmund, David James for alerting me to his and David Algar's work on Sorbiodunum, Peter Hart for information on the street names of Salisbury, Steve Hobbs for furnishing me with the Tisbury rent roll at the time of the Black Death, George Fleming for information on Salisbury in World War One and Norman Parker for information on Salisbury in World War Two, and Peter Riley for his assistance in locating images from the Edwin Young Collection. Last but by no means least I thank the residents and proprietors of properties which I have photographed or those from which I have been able to gain advantageous viewpoints. Thank you all.

Part One
A history of Salisbury

Chronology

Particularly significant dates are given in bold type.

Iron Age–Roman Conquest	(6th century BC–post-AD 68): fortified settlement at present-day Old Sarum.
Roman Era	(1st–5th century AD): Romano-British settlement at Sorbiodunum (Old Sarum), is identified by that name in the Antonine Itinerary (3rd–4th century AD).
552	**Saxons under Cynrig are victorious in battle at Searoburh (Old Sarum),** which continues as a fortified settlement during the early Middle Ages.
1066–1070	In the immediate aftermath of the Norman Conquest, Old Sarum is fortified anew.
1075	**Old Sarum becomes the seat of the new diocese, combined from the sees of Ramsbury and Sherborne.**
1078–1092	**The first Salisbury Cathedral is built at Old Sarum by Bishop St Osmund.**
1091	**Earliest mention of St Martin's Church, and of schooling arrangements for choristers (later to become the Cathedral School).**
*c.*1200	The site of the new town is determined.
1220	**Foundations of the cathedral are laid.**
1227	**Henry II grants the first charter to Salisbury, confirming the right to hold a weekly market, and granting the right to hold a fair in August.**
***c.*1240**	**Ayleswade Bridge is built by Bishop Bingham to cross the River Avon south of the city.**
1248	**Earliest mention of St Thomas's Church.**
1258	**The cathedral is consecrated.**
1266	**The cathedral is completed.**
1269	**St Edmund's Church is founded by Bishop Walter de la Wyle.**
1313–1334	**The spire is built.**
1335	Earliest mention of the Poultry Cross, the sole survivor of the city's four ancient market crosses (the present building dates from the 15th century).
1483	Henry, Duke of Buckingham, is executed for rebellion against Richard III.
1556	Charles, Lord Stourton, is hanged with a silken cord for murder; Maundrel, Spicer and Coberly are burnt at the stake for heresy.
1579–1584	The city fathers build their Council House, predecessor to the present Guildhall.
1612	**James I grants the city fathers a charter of incorporation.**
1625	Charles I and his court stay in Salisbury to avoid the plague.
1627	**Mayor Ivie saves Salisbury from the worst effects of the plague.**
1645	The 'Battle of Salisbury', the only such engagement between parliamentary and royalist forces to take place during the Civil War.
1653	Anne Bodenham is executed for witchcraft.

1654	John Evelyn visits Salisbury.
1655	Col. John Penruddock, leading a royalist rebellion, kidnaps the Assize judges and frees the prisoners from the gaol; later he is captured and executed.
1665	Charles II and his court stay in Salisbury to avoid the plague.
1668	Samuel Pepys stays at the George Inn; Sir Christopher Wren visits Salisbury at Bishop Ward's invitation to undertake a structural survey of the cathedral.
1688	Salisbury is the headquarters of James II at the time of the Glorious Revolution, but welcomes William of Orange (later King William III) on his way from Torbay to Oxford.
1715	Salisbury's first newspaper, the ***Salisbury Post Man***, is launched; it ceases publication after a few issues. George I visits the city.
1729	**The *Salisbury Journal* is established.**
1740	Earliest mention of the music festivals, taking place annually on St Cecilia's day.
1767	**The Infirmary is founded following a public appeal in the aftermath of a smallpox outbreak.**
1780	The Council House is seriously damaged by fire.
1784	Godolphin School for Girls is founded.
1788–1795	**Building of the Guildhall, the gift to the city of the Earl of Radnor.**
1789–1792	**Bishop Shute Barrington commissions the architect James Wyatt to landscape the Cathedral Close, remove late-mediaeval accretions to the cathedral's structure and to demolish the belfry.**
1792	George III and his family visit Salisbury.
1795	The Salisbury and Southampton Canal project is embarked upon; it is abandoned early in the next century.
1830	Agricultural workers in revolt wreck a threshing machine at Bishopdown; at the subsequent trial 28 are sentenced to transportation for life.
1832	The Great Reform Act withdraws the franchise from Old Sarum.
1833	**Street lighting by gas is introduced.**
1836	**Salisbury is incorporated under the Municipal Corporations Act. City police force is established, remaining an independent force until 1946.**
1841	**Diocesan teacher training college for women is established in the Close.**
1847	**Inauguration of Salisbury's first rail transport link – with Southampton.**
1849	**Cholera epidemic reaches Salisbury.**
1851	Prince Albert visits Salisbury.
1852	Floods in the city leave Fisherton Street submerged. Salisbury's Exhibition of Art, Industry and Antiquities is staged in the Guildhall.
1855	The last public hanging takes place at the junction of Wilton and Devizes Roads.
1855–1875	The open watercourses – which had given to Salisbury the epithet 'The English Venice' – are drained, cleared and filled in, and succeeded by a modern underground drainage system. The artefacts recovered from the watercourses form the nucleus of the Salisbury and South Wiltshire Museum.
1856	Queen Victoria and her family visit Salisbury.
1859	**The Market House is opened.**
1861	**The Tintometer company is founded by J.W. Lovibond, to produce chemical analysis apparatus based on colour. Salisbury and South Wiltshire Museum is opened in Castle Street.**
1862–1879	**Restoration of the cathedral under Sir George Gilbert Scott.**
1868	**The *Salisbury Times* is established.**
1871	**Hamilton Hall is opened in New Street, as the home of the Literary and Scientific Institution, and from 1875, the School of Art.**

1883	The Green Croft is restored to the city as a public open space by Revd Dr G.H. Bourne.
1887	Victoria Park is opened to commemorate the Queen's Golden Jubilee.
1890	**Adoption of the Public Libraries Act: the first city library is opened in Endless Street. Bishop Wordsworth's School is opened.**
1902	Salisbury's only motor manufacturer, Scout Motors Ltd, is formed; goes bankrupt in 1921.
1905	New, purpose-built city library is opened in Chipper Lane, funded by the philanthropist Andrew Carnegie. The first Salisbury staging of the Southern Cathedrals Festival (inaugurated at Chichester in 1904).
1906	**Rail disaster in which 28 people are killed when the Boat Train leaves the rails while passing through Salisbury station.**
1908	Cinema arrives in Salisbury with the showing of a film in the County Hall. A dedicated cinema is opened in Fisherton Street in 1916.
1915	Floods in the city leave Fisherton Street and the Close submerged. Cecil Chubb buys Stonehenge, part of the Antrobus family estates, at auction in Salisbury; in 1918 he presents the landmark and its environs to the nation, for which he is granted a baronetcy.
1922	City War Memorial is unveiled in the Market Place by Lt Tom Adlam, Salisbury's VC.
1927	**Salisbury City Council offices move from the Guildhall to Bourne Hill, the former home of the Wyndham family in Salisbury, and the bequest to the city of the Revd Dr Bourne. South Wilts Secondary School for Girls (later the Grammar School) is opened.**
1935	**Ayleswade Bridge, which has carried traffic to the south of the city since *c.*1240, is replaced by a new road bridge to the east.**
1940–42	Salisbury suffers minor damage in five air raids, the only such instances of the war.
1950	**Salisbury Arts Theatre (now the Playhouse) is established.**
1959	**Salisbury's first purpose-built cattle market is opened.**
1962–1969	**Inner ring road is built.**
1967	Salisbury's first Festival of the Arts is staged.
1969	**Salisbury's first shopping precinct, the Old George Mall, is opened.**
1973	**The annual series of Festivals of the Arts is inaugurated.**
1974	**The Plume of Feathers Inn on Queen Street and adjacent buildings in the Cross Keys Chequer are redeveloped as the Cross Keys shopping mall. The Queen visits Salisbury.**
1975	**Salisbury Library is opened on the site of the Market House.**
1976	**Salisbury Playhouse is opened on the site of former malthouses.**
1982	**Salisbury Arts Centre is opened in the redundant church of St Edmund.**
1986	The Law Courts are transferred from the Guildhall to purpose-built accommodation in the former NAAFI building.
1987–1993	**The cathedral spire is restored.**
1991	The Prince and Princess of Wales visit Salisbury to attend the Symphony for the Spire gala concert.
1993	**New Salisbury District Hospital is opened at Odstock; the Infirmary in Fisherton Street is closed for residential redevelopment.**
1993–1994	Salisbury by-pass enquiry.
1995	Old George Mall is redeveloped.
1996	New livestock market is opened on Netherhampton Road
1997	Incoming Labour Government scraps plans for a by-pass. Waitrose out-of-town superstore is opened on the site of the old livestock market.
2001	Salisbury's first park-and-ride scheme is opened near Old Sarum.

Chapter 1
The Accursed Hill

SALISBURY'S story begins with its name; and thus, the history of the city dates back over 1,500 years before the foundation of the settlement we now recognise by the name of Salisbury. The first Salisbury was probably a settlement or group of settlements adjacent to and under the protection of a hill fort built perhaps as early as 600 BC, and probably no later than 300 BC, during the Iron Age. The whole of the surrounding area bears witness to human occupation and activity for thousands of years before that Iron-Age hill fort was built, but there are compelling reasons for the fortification of that particular spot.

The Origins

Old Sarum, as we now know the hill fort, was built on a spur of chalk upland on the southernmost edge of Salisbury Plain: the lie of the land, which drops away sharply to the north, the south and the west, provided the Celtic settlers with a natural fortress requiring little beyond the construction of a ditch-and-rampart system to complete the fortifications. The hill fort overlooked the fertile river valleys of the Bourne and the Avon, navigable as far as the sea, and stood at the junction of a number of ancient trackways. Running eastwards is the Lunway, believed to have been so named because ultimately it led to London. Adjoining the Lunway at Old Sarum's East Gate are two routes striking northwards. The westerly route traverses the river valleys and skirts the Plain until it reaches Yarnbury Castle, another major Iron-Age hill fort and a trading centre until modern times, while the northerly route crosses the Plain to Everleigh, Easton and Ram Alley, near Burbage, where it links with the road to Marlborough. The discovery of a bronze belt-link at Old Sarum suggests trading ties with the West Country, and indeed the western slope of the promontory overlooks both the Avon and the crossing point for traders and travellers westwards. Other finds, such as coinage of the chieftains Tasciovanus and Cunobelinus, indicate the presence of the Belgae, but only with the arrival of the Romans and the entry of the hill fort's name into the historical

Old Sarum. The view is from the east, with the farmhouse at Ford in the foreground, and the cluster of Stratford-sub-Castle to the left, and is from Hall's ***Picturesque memorials of Salisbury***, 1834. Cobbett, travelling down the Avon Valley in 1826, described the hill fort's appearance as three cheeses, 'laid one upon the other; the bottom a great deal broader than the next, and the top one like a Stilton cheese in proportion to a Gloucester one'.

record as Sorbiodunum, in the fourth-century Antonine Itinerary, do we have evidence of its identity in the Iron Age. For '*Sorbiodunum*' is simply a Latinisation of two Celtic place-name elements, of which the first is a slow-moving stream and the second is a fortified place.

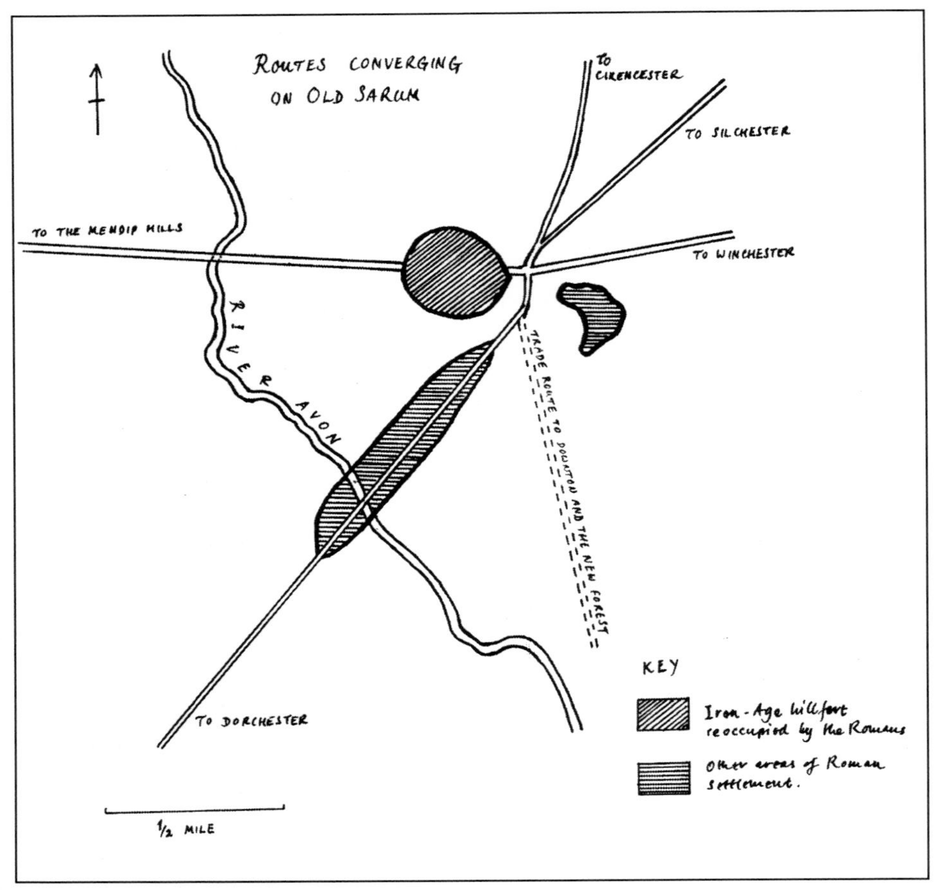

Routes converging on Old Sarum.

Romans and Saxons

That in Roman times Old Sarum continued to be of importance can again be deduced from the layout of the roads converging on the site. Running east is the road to Winchester, and west, the road to the lead mines of the Mendips. Diagonally across this route is the Portway, running north-east to Silchester and south-west to Dorchester. Apart from these routes of both military and economic importance, ancient trackways served local trades, and it has been surmised that pottery from the New Forest arrived via Downton and Petersfinger on a trading route to the eastern entrance of the hill fort. The question remains open whether the Romano-British settlement lay solely within the confines of the ancient hill fort, or was developed immediately to the west, at present-day Stratford-sub-Castle, but the latter possibility seems more likely given the Saxon naming of the point at which the Roman road crossed the river. The most recent research indicates a strong possibility that Sorbiodunum was not merely one of the hundreds of fortified garrison stations with or without an adjacent civilian community, but a substantial settlement – an ***oppidum***. The evidence of finds suggests the presence of two main quarters along the line of the Portway, south of the hill fort, and to the east of the eastern entrance to the hill fort, as well as the suburb at Bishopdown. On this evidence it has been postulated that Sorbiodunum was a local administrative, market and industrial centre and a way-station for the trading traffic from the east Dorset coast, its hinterland and the New Forest up to Silchester and London. Given its importance to another group of invaders a millennium later, again characterised by military and administrative prowess sufficient to outweigh paucity of numbers, we should not be surprised to learn of Sorbiodunum's value to the Romans. Judging by the area of the settlements, at around 100 acres, Sorbiodunum can appropriately be considered as one of the 'small towns' of Roman Britain.

With the passing of the Romans, the settlement once more sank into obscurity, illuminated only by the almost mythical events described in the ***Anglo-Saxon Chronicle***. The pattern of invasions begun in the Bronze Age and continued by the Belgae and the Romans was repeated by the Saxons, with engagements between the British and the Saxons under Cerdic, at Charford near Downton, in 519. When his son, Cynric, was victorious

Pennies from the Old Sarum Mint. Top row: Canute: obverse; William I, obverse; bottom row: William I, reverse: moneyer: Godwin; Canute, reverse: moneyer: Saeman.

in battle against the British in 552, the scene of that victory was again adapted to the language of the incomers. The second element in the name, ***-dunum***, became ***-burh***, maintaining the meaning of a town or a fortified place, but the first element, ***Sorbio***, or ***Sarva***, was altered to ***Searo***, meaning a battle, or a trick – possibly an ambush – hence ***Searoburh***, which became, with the passage of time, ***Sarisberia*** and then Salisbury. ('Sarum', enshrined in the name of the original hill fort site and later rotten borough, and in the official name of the city corporation until 1974, arises, like the word 'viz', from the mispronunciation of a shortening of the town's name by scribes in the Middle Ages). It appears that when the locality was settled by the Saxons, their preference was for communities and farmsteads in the river valleys, with the uplands – including the enclosures which had served both as places of refuge and centres of trade – being reserved for sheep-farming. However, as Saxon civilisation developed in the area, and its wealth proved attractive to a further wave of invaders, the Place of Battle again assumed a strategic importance.

The West Saxons had settled upon Wilton as their provincial capital, but it was King Alfred who set the seal on the town's status and development, firstly by including Wilton in the Burghal Hideage, the list of towns throughout his realm which were to serve as strongholds in the event of invasion, and secondly by adding to the endowments of the nunnery founded in 800. Its importance can be inferred from the presence of a royal palace and a minster church as well as the nunnery, which survived until the Dissolution, and whose royal associations continued when Edith, half-sister to Edward the Martyr and Ethelred the Unready, chose to live and die there. Despite its importance, Wilton was vulnerable: it was sacked after the eponymous battle in 871, and again in 1003, during the Danish King Sweyn Forkbeard's campaign to avenge Ethelred's massacre of his countrymen, and indeed his sister, the previous year.

At that point, the moneyers of the royal mint decamped to the safety of Salisbury, which had been refortified by King Alfred, its ditch being re-dug and its ramparts lined with palisades. It had also been the venue for a court of King Edgar, convened to discuss the defence of the realm, and it retained a mint from 1003 until the reign of Henry II (1154–89), and it seems likely that Salisbury was redeveloped to serve as the stronghold for Wilton.

After the Conquest

At the Conquest of 1066 Salisbury's strategic value was again appreciated, the more so, perhaps, because of the relatively small numbers of the new governing class, and the consequent need to make the most effective use of the available manpower. It must have been immediately apparent that the site – like, for example, Portchester in Hampshire – would lend itself to redevelopment as a typical motte-and-bailey castle, for a mound was raised in the highest, central point of the enclosure, surmounted by a timber keep as early as 1070. References in contemporary sources point to William's presence at Salisbury within a very few years of the Conquest (unsurprisingly in view of the building of a royal palace in the nearby Forest of Clarendon), and of his son and grandson. The timber structure was soon replaced by a stone keep, and the ditch-and-rampart system re-dug, and surmounted by a curtain wall. It is believed that the results of the Domesday Survey were presented to the king at Salisbury in 1086, much of the information having been collated there under the direction of Bishop Osmund, sometime Chancellor to the king. The castle was the venue in the same year, on 1 August, for the council at which the major landowners rendered homage to the king. There can be no doubt, then, of

Salisbury's importance in the early Norman period, as a royal castle rather than a township, continuing a pattern of use from the late Saxon period. William of Malmesbury refers to Salisbury as the castle, being ***juris proprium*** of the king, while Florence of Worcester describes the new cathedral church as being built within the castle. It might seem that from the moment of its conception the notion of siting the administrative centre of a diocese within a military complex was doomed, but two cathedrals were built there within the space of a century. It was thus by no means a foregone conclusion that Salisbury would only survive with a fresh start in a new location – it could well have developed outside the castle walls.

Borough and Diocese

The decision to centre the diocese within the castle may have appeared as curious at the time as it does with the benefit of hindsight, but in fact the diocese and the location of the seat of the bishopric at Salisbury are the result of historical accident. Herman, remembered today as Salisbury's first bishop, but at one time chaplain to Edward the Confessor, was promoted to the Bishopric of Ramsbury in 1045. The appointment was not a success, however, and the bishop left to enter the monastery at St Omer – without, however, resigning his bishopric. When he was invited, in 1058, to become Bishop of Sherborne, he never surrendered Ramsbury. The adjacent sees were combined into one, which thus covered an enormous area from Dorset to Berkshire.

Herman held his combined diocese after 1066, but was to be directly affected by the Norman policy of basing episcopal jurisdictions not on relatively small communities, as had been the Saxon custom, but on towns. The Council of London in 1075 put this policy into effect, and Herman was ordered to transfer his seat to Salisbury, as a central point for the new diocese, and adjacent to manorial estates held by the bishop in the Avon valley immediately to the south. It is probably this factor which explains the choice of Salisbury rather than, say, Wilton or Amesbury. And, although the cathedral was indeed built within the bailey, the area within the ramparts amounted to almost 30 acres, and about half of the area of the bailey was given over to the cathedral precincts.

The endowments for the cathedral chapter included income from Stratford-sub-Castle and the land near the castle gate.

The First Cathedral at Salisbury

The new cathedral was built to a plan common throughout the Norman world, having an apse and transepts taking the form of apsidal chapels. The design has echoes of La Trinité at Caen and this aspect, together with the building's modest scale, places it firmly behind the van of post-Conquest English cathedral building. At around 185ft long, the cathedral was some 120ft shorter than the Old Minster at Winchester, completed some 80 years earlier, and was easily the smallest of the English Norman cathedrals. It seems that Herman was not an ambitious builder, despite the resources at his disposal, and was content with a cathedral on a scale appropriate for an Anglo-Saxon bishopric – like, for example, that at Sherborne, believed to have been about the same size as the first Salisbury cathedral. However, that cathedral had a life scarcely beyond the imagination of its founder, who died within three years of the move to Salisbury, or his successor, Osmund, for no sooner had it been consecrated in 1092 than its eastern end was struck by lightning and practically destroyed in the ensuing storm. Osmund's more enduring legacies included, on the one hand, the creation of a library of which over 50 volumes are still to be found in the present cathedral library, and on the other, a life of charity, piety and miracles, leading to his canonisation in 1457. Arguably more important than either of these was his codification of religious practice now known as the Sarum Use.

The Use of Sarum is a collective title for the constitution of the cathedral chapter at Salisbury, the directions for conducting the services and the texts of the rites for the various services. The Sarum Use was widely adopted throughout Great Britain and Ireland, and influenced liturgical developments throughout western Christendom up to and beyond the Reformation. As regards the organisation of the church, in detailing how a secular chapter was to be constituted and run, the Use of Sarum established one of the three main models for the life of the church – the others being the orders of monks and of friars – in the era before the Reformation. Following the dissolution of the monasteries and the refounding of many cathedral chapters within the

The Use of Sarum. A page from a breviary (a personal service-book) according to the Sarum Use. The page shown is from an edition printed in black and red, produced in London by John Kyngston and Henry Sutton in 1555, and is a calendar for the month of February, showing the saints' days celebrated with a prescription of the order of service to be followed.

Church of England, it is the secular model, comprising a body of canons having their own accommodation, and led by four principal officers, the dean, the precentor, the chancellor and the treasurer, which has survived to this day. So to observe the life of a modern cathedral chapter, or to attend a service whether at a cathedral or a parish church, is in key respects to witness the Use of Sarum to this day.

An Over-reaching Bishop

Saint Osmund was succeeded by Roger of Caen, as unlike Osmund as possible, a man whose vigour in the exercise of temporal power created an impression more typical of a prince-bishop of a much later era. And therein, arguably, lies the explanation for the eventual decline and ultimate abandonment of the mediaeval borough of Salisbury. Roger had risen from humble origins in Avranches through the ranks of the clergy at a time when links between the Church and the State enabled success in the one sphere to be translated into preferment in the other. The worldly prelate, who kept one Matilda of Ramsbury for his mistress, is said to have commended himself to the first Henry's attention by his ability to rush through the celebration of the Mass to allow the king all the more time for hunting. On Henry's accession in 1100, the royal chaplain was appointed Chancellor of England, having already attained the offices of chief justiciar and treasurer; in 1102 he was elected to the bishopric of Salisbury, although he was not consecrated until 1107.

The first of Roger's considerable architectural ambitions was the rebuilding of Herman's cathedral. Taking as his pattern the Abbaye aux Dames at Caen, he endowed it with a greatly extended nave and a tower above the crossing, and an extended and square-ended east end; twin towers flanking the west front were to complete the design. The first cathedral, at just under 200ft in length, broke no new ground in the scale of its execution, but Roger's was almost 100ft longer, and comparable in size with those at Bristol, Hereford or Rochester. Had it survived, even as a Norman building, it would have been a formidable symbol of the Church Militant, and William of Malmesbury marvelled at the quality of the ashlared stonework, declaring that the cathedral appeared to have been fashioned from a single block of stone. The second Salisbury cathedral was distinguished not only by the quality of its stonework, but also by its decoration, still to be savoured from excavated specimens now in the Salisbury and South Wiltshire Museum and from fragments in the Close wall, their presence resulting from the earlier cathedral's final fate as a quarry for building in the new city. The sculptor is anonymous, and thus simply identified as the Old Sarum Master. The extent of his influence can be gauged by the presence of more of his work at All Saints', Lullington (Somerset) and St Swithun's, Leonard Stanley (Gloucestershire), and his vigorous and exuberant style inspired the Herefordshire School whose work can be seen at Kilpeck and Shobdon.

Roger added further to the cathedral complex, by building a treasury immediately to the north of the north transept, a cloister between it and the chancel, and a palace between the cloister and the circumference of the hill fort site, on which he built a substantial

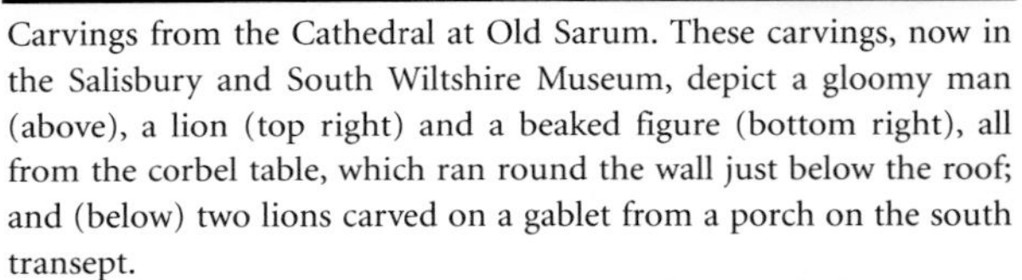

Carvings from the Cathedral at Old Sarum. These carvings, now in the Salisbury and South Wiltshire Museum, depict a gloomy man (above), a lion (top right) and a beaked figure (bottom right), all from the corbel table, which ran round the wall just below the roof; and (below) two lions carved on a gablet from a porch on the south transept.

Old Sarum Castle. This completely fanciful impression is perhaps derived from or inspired by the tomb brass to Bishop Robert de Wyville (1330–1375) in Salisbury Cathedral. Making due allowances for artistic licence, the fortifications probably bore some resemblance to Roger of Caen's castles at Sherborne and Devizes; the association of Wyville and the castle arises from his recovery of Sherborne Castle.

curtain wall. Sometime around 1130, Roger was appointed castellan at Salisbury, and the extent of his secular authority and ambitions may be gauged by his building of castles at Malmesbury, Devizes and Sherborne. The only representation of the castle of Salisbury is fanciful in the extreme, but the remains of Sherborne Castle give a rough idea of Salisbury's appearance. Meanwhile the town developed as a commercial centre, helped by Bishop Roger's granting to the burgesses the right to hold an annual fair, and exemption from tolls.

The death of Henry I, the civil war between the supporters of Henry's daughter, Matilda, and his nephew Stephen, and the 19 winters of Stephen's reign spelt doom for Roger, and, ultimately, for the Borough of Salisbury. Roger had reneged on his support for Matilda, but his loyalty to Stephen's cause was sufficiently compromised for Stephen to commandeer the castles, imprison the bishop and seize the treasure he had amassed for the further development of the cathedral. The harshness of his imprisonment and the circumstances of his disgrace (his nephews, bishops of Ely and Lincoln, had simultaneously been arrested) probably contributed to his death from fever in the year of his downfall, 1139.

The Decision to Move

Once the castellancy reverted to the military authorities, Bishop Roger's fortifications at Salisbury served only to constrain the bishops and the cathedral chapter. Although development continued in the communities outside the walls, the ongoing disharmony between the religious and military communities within the fortified borough rendered the life of the cathedral untenable. Later monarchs had no particular interest in Salisbury, and many of the troops garrisoned there were mercenaries. On the one hand the lack of military discipline led to perennial disturbances between the soldiers and the clergy, and on the other, there were curtailments of clerical liberties by the castellan in areas of life ranging from availability of water to freedom of movement. Then, in 1217, the canons of the cathedral went out to St Martin's Church on a Rogationtide procession, and on returning to Salisbury found their entry barred. In the laconic words of the ***Tropenell Cartulary***, '***Set ministri regis nullum intrare permiserunt***' – 'But the king's officers allowed no-one to enter'.

In the mediaeval narrative this event is portrayed as the straw which broke the camel's back, prompting the new bishop, Richard Poore, to lend his weight to his dean and chapter's appeal to Pope Honorius III for permission to undertake the move to the site by the river. Thenceforth events moved relatively swiftly to the consecration of the site and the building of a wooden chapel in 1219, and the laying of the foundation stones in April 1220. In fact, a decision in principle had been taken over 20 years earlier, when, with the support of Hubert Walter, Archbishop of Canterbury and a former Bishop of Salisbury, King Richard the Lionheart's assent had been granted. And there matters lay during the troubled reign of King John, for five years of which, from 1208 to 1213, England lay under a papal interdict. The political uncertainties of the last years of Richard's reign, with far worse to follow, as well as possible concerns about the cost of the venture, were justification enough for Herbert Poore's caution, despite the strictures of the author of the ***Register of St Osmund***, who accused him of failing to meet the challenge like troops prepared and armed who yet turn back on the day of battle.

The papal bull of 1218 granting permission for the move cites a number of grounds on which the petition was accepted: the constraints bordering on house arrest imposed by the military authorities, the increasing dilapidation of the cathedral, the cost of its upkeep and the decline in the congregation, and the inadequacy of the water supplies. Other more fanciful complaints were that the site was lashed by winds which shook the cathedral and drowned the clerks' voices at holy service, and that with neither grass nor trees, the clerks were dazzled by the bare chalk, some to the point of blindness. These tribulations are echoed in a contemporary poem by Henry of Avranches, who added:

Mons salisberie, quasi Gelboe mons maledictus,
Est inter montes, sicut et illa fuit.
...Ventus ibi clamat, sed phylomena silet.

As Gilboa was accursed among mountains,
So likewise was the hill of Salisbury.
...There the wind howls, but the nightingale is silent.

So many contemporary sources recount the story of the

events leading to the new city's foundation that today it seems inevitable – but was this really the case? Had the castellancy remained vested with the bishops of Salisbury, it is by no means beyond the bounds of possibility that a cathedral quarter might have continued to develop at Old Sarum. Precincts such as Durham and Lincoln were successfully developed on sites quite as exposed as Old Sarum's, and the presence of Shaftesbury, about 20 miles to the west, overlooking an escarpment and having an area broadly comparable with Old Sarum's 30 acres, gives an impression of what Salisbury would have been like. As at Shaftesbury, described erroneously as 'waterless', there were wells both within the precincts and within 100 yards of the ramparts. There was a flourishing commercial quarter just outside the ramparts, and one can imagine how a new quarter like Carcassonne's Bastide St Louis might have developed below the old town. A third cathedral at the hill fort, on the levelled site of the keep, would at once have had a precinct to compare with Winchester's, and been visible, like Ely or Chartres, from many miles away.

However, behind the rhetoric of whistling winds and dazzling chalk lay a quiet determination, born of reasoned economic assessment, nurtured in a womb of oppression for 50 years, and raised for a further 25 years of planning and building away to the south. The real reasons for the proposed move were these. There were too few houses for the canons, and others had to be acquired from the townsfolk for there was no room to build any more: those that they had were in the quarter near the east gate and thus not especially convenient for the cathedral precinct, in the north-west quadrant of the enclosure. The cathedral itself was small and old-fashioned in appearance, and in its present location no further development was possible: in the changed situation after Roger's death, Bishop Jocelyn's narthex at the west end completed the building. Elsewhere, however, other cathedrals outshone Salisbury: Winchester was half as long again, Durham, high on a bluff overlooking the River Wear, was 400ft long, as was Ely. Major rebuildings, such as at Canterbury and Wells, were coming to fruition. Down by the river, just north of a crossing known as Ayleswade, land belonging to the bishop had already been earmarked for development, ever since permission had been gained from King Richard, and it was decreed in 1213 exactly where the canons were to build their residences in the area identified to become the Close. In 1219, Bishop Poore granted the right of holding a market to the new community, which was by then clearly more than a village; in due course the burgesses of the old borough were to protest at the competition of their new neighbour. But consideration of these developments belongs to the next chapter.

Decline and Fall

Meanwhile, at Salisbury, soon to be known for ever as Old Sarum, life continued, although there was a gradual decline in the borough's fortunes and importance, which can be measured down the centuries by certain key events. At various points in the new century the conventual buildings were ordered to be demolished to provide material for the maintenance of the castle and the dean and chapter were granted the cathedral as building material, which can be seen to this day in the walls of the Close. As the strategic importance of the castle declined, so it was converted into a gaol; one so poorly maintained, however, that in 1305 20 prisoners were able to break out, carrying off a quantity of royal treasure as they left. By 1535, when Leland visited the site, it was deserted: the castle in ruins and no trace of the cathedral. Occasionally there was a flicker of resurgence: the borough may briefly have been a royal mint during the Civil War. Otherwise Old Sarum's life was limited to that of a curiosity for visitors, possibly because of its continuing existence as a political entity – a rotten borough representing a pocketful of electors, and behind them powerful vested interests. Perhaps its final glory was its association with William Pitt the Elder, its most distinguished Parliamentary representative. Its final epitaph from that era, echoing Henry of Avranches, was Cobbett's description of August 1826 from the ***Rural Rides***, as 'the Accursed Hill'.

Chapter 2

'Let us in God's name descend into the plain'

IT WAS to the great good fortune of the cathedral that the new city and the close were planned along trade routes, and with the benefits of trade in mind. For the line of the path from Old Sarum, across the fordable stretch of the Avon to an ancient trackway along the ridge of Harnham Hill, was to become the spine of the city and to run through the heart of the Close. Whether it was done knowingly or unwittingly, the laying of the cathedral's foundation stones within a few yards of that north-south route was to have inestimable benefits from a civil engineering perspective.

However, the key decision in assuring the cathedral's future was that of creating a town: a centre of trade and hence of industry, to support the work of the cathedral. No matter how much appeals for funding might raise for the construction of the church and its associated buildings, there had to be a steady source of revenue for their upkeep and for the life of the principal church in the diocese. Monastic foundations relied upon huge endowments of land, and the income accruing from farming, but the lands held by the Bishop of Salisbury were nowhere near as extensive. Instead, while doubtless suggested by a realisation of how a cathedral chapter could be supported by trade from experience at Old Sarum, and by seeing the success of new towns elsewhere, the Poore brothers' resolution to refound Salisbury was as audacious as it was shrewd.

Mediaeval New Towns – a National Trend

The founding of the new city – as, indeed, the development of Old Sarum two centuries earlier – can be viewed as part of a national trend. The earlier development arose from the determination of the late Saxon kings to build and strengthen their realm, and the corresponding upsurge after the Conquest can be seen in a similar light. Thus, during the years between the Conquest and 1130, some 58 new towns were established throughout England and Wales: in Wiltshire nine new towns other than Salisbury were founded in the 13th century. Although at the outset many boroughs were royal foundations, and were created to reinforce the Norman hegemony, by the time Salisbury was established most new towns were founded by the nobility or senior clerics, with economic, not political objectives. Bishop Roger had refounded Devizes a few decades before, while Peter de Roches, Bishop of Winchester, had similarly refounded Downton in 1208; he had also founded Hindon from scratch in 1219.

What was to ensure Salisbury's success, however, was not simply that the town enjoyed command of important trade routes – just as did Wilton and Old Sarum – the better to support the life and work of the cathedral. It was, as John Chandler has pointed out, that with a great cathedral, the subject of planning every bit as careful as the city's, Salisbury would never lack visitors – pilgrims initially, tourists nowadays – to be welcomed and boarded. In a symbiotic relationship, rents and dues from the city would support the cathedral, and the cathedral would draw wealth into the city. The idea of founding a new city and a new cathedral simultaneously may have been suggested to Bishop Poore by the example of Lichfield, whose Saxon cathedral had been rebuilt a century earlier, and a new town established at the same time.

The Site of the New City

The choice of the land on which to build the new city and the cathedral was as axiomatic in the 12th century, when it was a greenfield site, as it would seem with the

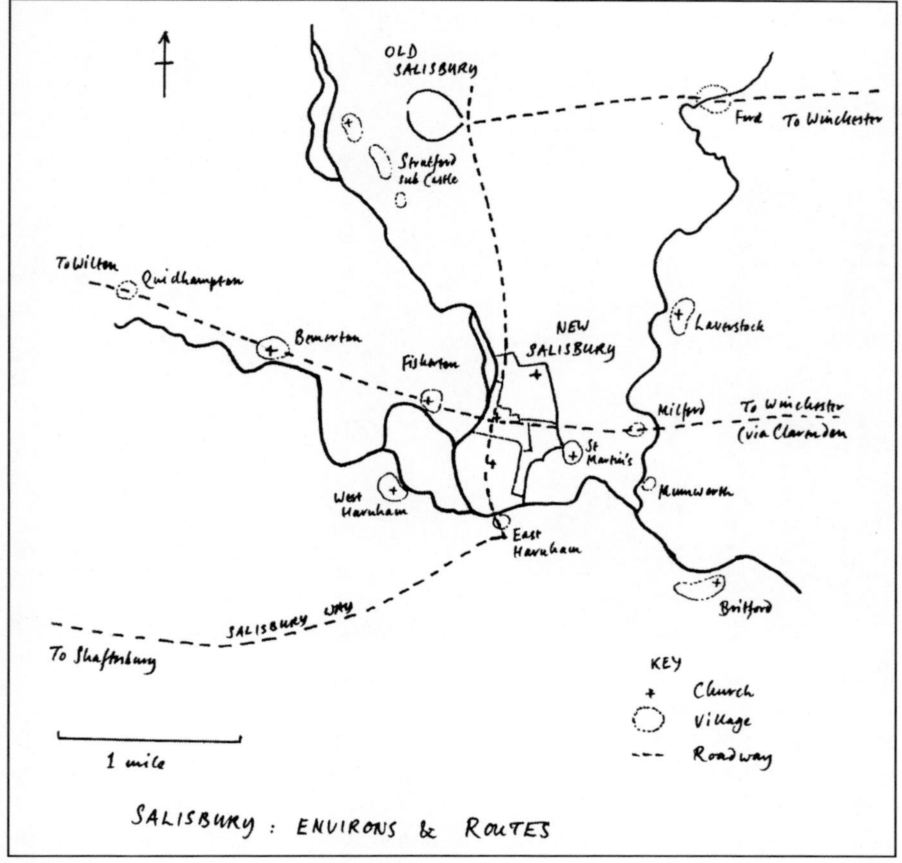

Salisbury and immediate environs, plus routes.

benefit of hindsight. This stretch of territory, with the Avon partially navigable to the sea, with a direct route, parallel to the Avon, linking Old Sarum and its routes with the ancient highway to the West Country, and with the Nadder joining the Avon and both providing motive power – all this potential for the creation of wealth – was already the bishop's. The area was already home to a number of established communities, which may themselves have provided pointers to the viability of any new urban development. Just as today there are villages along the valleys of the five rivers which meet in and around Salisbury, there would have been some settlements between Stratford-sub-Castle and Harnham, of which all traces have vanished beneath Salisbury's streets. But there were also parishes such as Fisherton and the area around St Martin's Church, and smaller communities at Milford and Petersfinger. Collectively they were known as the Old Salisburies – in a bull of 1146, in which Pope Eugenius III confirms gifts of land to the Bishop of Salisbury they are so described; in Latin as ***veteres Sarisberias.*** And so it would have seemed to the inhabitants at the time, for then the suburbs around the castle gates were recent developments. That this notion of two Salisburies, old and new, was long accepted before ever the new city was planned is borne out by references in the Domesday Survey. There is the area called Salisbury – and a very extensive area at that – on which the bishop paid taxes, which is quite distinct from the Salisbury (latter-day Old Sarum) which is included among the boroughs and borough-like communities whose inhabitants were liable for the 'third penny' tax.

Exactly where the cathedral – and thus the new city – was to be placed is the stuff of legend. The ***Tropenell Cartulary's*** record of the founding of Salisbury describes how Bishop Poore, having been granted sanction to found the new cathedral, cast around for a suitable location, and initially pursued a scheme to relocate to Wilton. Gossip linking his name with that of the Abbess of Wilton caused him to reconsider: he laid the matter before Almighty God and the Blessed Virgin Mary, who promptly appeared in a dream and instructed the bishop to build the cathedral in Mirifield. The dream was so vivid that the bishop awoke, offered thanks to the Lord and noted the location, though the name meant nothing to him. Shortly afterwards, Mirifield, or Mary-field, was identified as an actual meadow among the episcopal landholdings, where in due course the cathedral foundation stones were laid. Another legend has an archer shooting an arrow from the battlements of Old Sarum, and the arrow travelling a mile and a half to the south, its landfall marking the spot for the building of the cathedral. In reality, however, as we have seen, the decisions about where the cathedral was to be located had long been

Harnham Gate. The wall to the north of the gate runs parallel to the route passing through the gate rather than at right angles, which suggests the gate is older than the wall, and may have been built for quite a different purpose, related to the house behind it rather than the Close wall.

taken, predicated already by the parcelling-out of plots for the canonries in what was later to become the Close, as far back as 1213. Peter of Blois declaimed 'Let us in God's name descend into the plain. There are rich champaign fields and fertile valleys, abounding with the fruits of the earth, and watered by the living stream. There is a seat for the Virgin patroness of our church to which the world cannot produce a parallel.' In so doing he was probably echoing a trend already under way. Thus, some properties would have been built by the time of the cathedral's foundation: the alignment of the Harnham Gate – parallel to the Close wall – suggests that it was a lodge gate for the canonry before ever there was any idea of enclosing the cathedral precincts with a curtain wall.

The Grand Design

In fact, several factors can be identified as coming together to shape the destiny of the grand design. Firstly, there was the area available to the bishop: south of Old Sarum and east of the River Avon, and north of the river when it curves to the east, north of Harnham. Then there is the lie of the land: absolutely flat in the present-day Close and the land to its east and directly to the north. Low-lying and poorly-drained – described at the time as a marsh for grazing animals – it was by no means prime farmland, although 400 years later, land such as this was turned into the agrarian power-house of the water meadows. The land on the west bank of the Avon did indeed become water-meadows, and afforded views of the cathedral immortalised by Constable and Turner. But in the 13th century, although the technology was available (for without it the new city would not have had its water supply), the idea had yet to surface, and hence this land, on the east bank of the river, could be surrendered without undue sacrifice in lost revenue from farming. The land east of the Close became the Friary, but in the 13th century it was undrained marshland.

The whole area was divided vertically by the road from Old Sarum to the Salisbury Way into two unequal portions, the narrower strip to the west bounded by the River Avon. It was divided again by an ancient road, originally from Winchester, which crossed the Avon at the site of the present-day Fisherton Bridge, just below the bishop's watermill. Were the integrity of these two routes to be maintained, it might be assumed that the 'city' quarter would be on either side of one or other of these routes, and the 'Close' quarter within one of the right angles formed by the crossing of the roads. Clearly, the two areas west of the road from Old Sarum to

Harnham, bounded by the Avon, were too narrow to offer a basis for development, and it follows that the divide between city and Close had to be a north-south division. The two areas – one within the crook of the Avon, the other, to the north, along the line of the east-west route towards the bishop's mill – were each self-evidently suited to their allotted function.

Salisbury Cathedral from across the Water Meadows. This classic view, and variations on it, have been essayed by painters, engravers and photographers from at least the time of Constable and Turner.

One of the complaints, it will be recalled, about Old Sarum, was the lack of water, and in the location and layout of a new city the importance of a plentiful and accessible water supply stands to reason. In fact the provision of watercourses as a feature of mediaeval urban planning can be observed in many towns and cities, both near and far from Salisbury, from nearby Wilton and Stockbridge to Frome or Cambridge, Rouen or Freiburg. But rarely was a scheme as carefully worked out as at Salisbury, drawing water from the Avon, and routing it through the streets through systems on two levels to rejoin the river beyond Bugmore Meadows, and earning for the city the soubriquet of the English Venice.

The Close

The area now contained within the Close enjoyed advantages both practical and aesthetic. Firstly, it was an enormous space, of about 83 acres – almost three times that of the enclosed area at Old Sarum. It was almost perfectly flat – the variation in the height above sea-level is a couple of feet only. The land appears to have been a common, and was thus an open space. The course of the river allowed for extensive grounds to the canonries facing the West Walk, which were the larger properties, reserved for the senior members of the chapter. It was intended that these properties be built on a grand scale: they had to provide accommodation for the canons' vicars-choral, and the South Canonry, for example, had its own chapel, plus a bakery, brewhouse and dovecot, as well as stables. Another early example was Leadenhall, built by Elias of Dereham from 1221, both to serve as his own home and as a specimen for other canonries.

Properties such as these indicate the position in society which the canons held, and, indeed, were expected to maintain, for it was a condition of their appointment that they develop their sites at their own expense. Many canons were wealthy landowners, and in addition enjoyed the income from their prebendal estates. Yet although the canonry plots had been allocated as far back as 1199, within the next quarter-century progress was slow, for in 1222 the chapter charged all with an empty plot to begin building by the following Whitsun, or else suffer forfeiture. Despite their station in life, however, few canons could afford to maintain an additional household, especially one which might not have been their principal residence, and thus over time the canonries largely reverted to the dean and chapter, to be leased to the cathedral clergy.

Even so, the houses in the Close proved too expensive for most of the clergy, and even before the Reformation, many had been let to wealthy lay folk, and thus, from early in the life of the new cathedral, its Close had the character of a quarter for well-to-do society in general – the already moneyed, rather than the rising merchant class represented by the likes of John Hall and William Swayne, who built in the city. By then, only seven of the Close houses remained as canonries. As

Ayleswade Bridge: A late 19th-century photograph (above) shows the Swan Inn, on the road from Coombe Bissett, while the view directly over the bridge (below), from the Lovibond Collection, shows the bridge in its last years as a through route. William Brown's pen-and-ink sketch (right) shows five of the bridge's spans on the west side over the Avon.

time passed, other uses were found for some Close properties, so that the situation today, in which there are three schools and two museums in the Close, is nothing new.

At the heart of the Close lay the cathedral, sited at the centre of the arc traced by the Avon. The road from Old Sarum marked the position of the west front of the cathedral, thus facilitating access for the primary building project. In fact the line of this road – and its loss as a through route once the close had been developed – was the one disadvantage to the Close site. That problem was surmounted with the creation of a new road, the later Exeter Street, running from the new town centre to the river-crossing, and involving a detour of

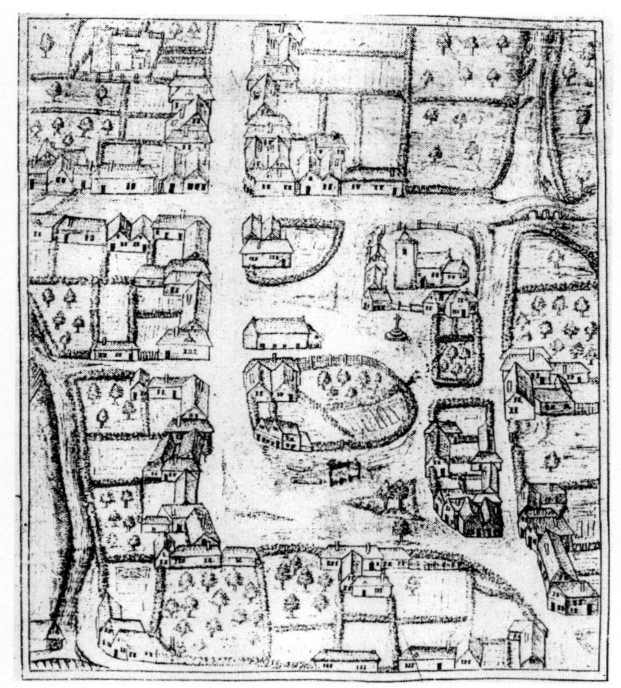

Wilton in 1568. The Market Place and environs are shown in this bird's-eye view from a survey of the Earl of Pembroke's lands, and it reveals, by the empty tenement plots, a town in decline by the mid-16th century.

about 100 yards. That the bishops, as landlords of the new centre of trade, were determined not to lose the advantage of the connection with the Old Salisbury Way, and thus ultimately with the western Ridgeway, can be inferred from the bridging of Aegel's Ford.

When in 1244 Bishop Bingham built the first Harnham Bridge, also known as Ayleswade Bridge, it was a deliberate pitch to draw traffic to and from the west into Salisbury and away from the river crossing at Wilton, Bull Bridge, and to generate income from levying of tolls. This event was not the turning point in Wilton's fortunes – its decline from being a regional capital to a satellite of Salisbury – for the reduction in 1230 of its taxation assessment by 25 per cent was a response to decades of decline, reversed only temporarily by the building of the new city. The extent of Wilton's ultimate decline can be seen in a bird's-eye view of the town in a survey of the Earl of Pembroke's lands of 1568, which depicts vacant plots around the Market Place (above).

At the time of its construction the bridge was no mean undertaking. The area was prone to flooding, to avoid which the project entailed the cutting of another channel, and building the bridge long enough to span both the river and the channel. On the eyot was built a little wayfarers' chapel dedicated to St John the Baptist. The nearby Hospital of St Nicholas, founded for the care of the sick and the needy among Salisbury's travellers, perhaps as long ago as 1227, was refounded with the additional remit of maintaining the chapel and the bridge. Its revenues, sourced from benefactions, were not sufficient for the upkeep of the bridge, and, to arrest its gradual dilapidation, the hospital was in 1413 granted the authority to raise the necessary funds by levying its own tolls on trade using the bridge. With widening in 1774, the bridge remained in service as part of the main southern route into the city until 1933.

These developments give a distinct impression of being the components of a planned community centred on the cathedral. That impression was reinforced by the foundation in 1262 of an academic college, that of the ***valle scholarum*** (rendered in Norman French as De Vaux College), for students exiled following disturbances at Oxford in 1238 and again between 1264 and 1278. The final development in the Close at this early stage was the building of the curtain wall, which today surrounds it on its northern, eastern and southern sides, and which succeeds a defensive ditch. Perhaps as a consequence of conflicts between the clergy and the laity, the Close was accorded the status and rights of sanctuary in 1317, and 10 years later, the king licensed the bishop to build a battlemented wall: its gatehouse into the city was at one time fortified with a portcullis. Work only began in 1331, when the king granted to the dean and chapter the right to re-use building materials from Old Sarum for that purpose (it having already been in use as a stone quarry for some decades previously). To this day, decorative carvings from the first cathedral, including roundels, arcading, rosettes, acanthus leaves and the odd corbel head can be spotted in the fabric of the Close wall.

The City

As for the city, the site at Poore's disposal amounted to some 180 acres, and, as with the cathedral, the guiding hand behind its layout is likely to have been Elias of Dereham. The initial plan may have been to develop the city along the line of the road from Winchester to the west via Wilton: the street between this route and the

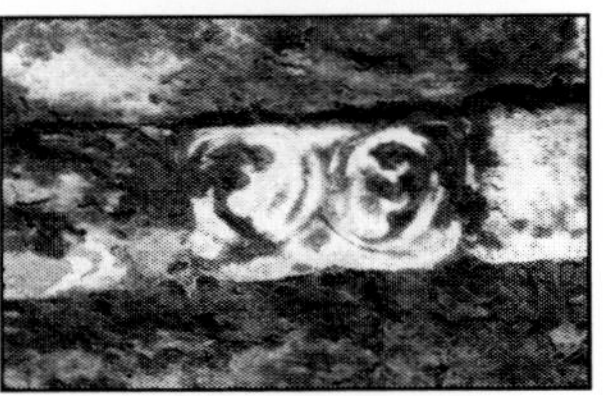

Stones from the Close Wall. These feature decorative elements from Old Sarum, probably from the cathedral, and include rosettes (left, above) and voussoirs (left, below), arcading (right, above) and acanthus leaves (right, below).

northern perimeter of the Close, and thus probably the first addition to the pre-existing road pattern, is called New Street. It linked to the settlement around St Martin's Church, which, incidentally, is referred to in contemporary sources as the church of St Martin ***in Salisbury***, indicating that the whole area from the Avon to the castle was thought of as Salisbury. The building on the southern corner of New Street with the High Street, Mitre House, lies, according to tradition, on the first plot of the new city to be developed. The grander design resulting in the grid plan we now have, however, must have been anticipated from a very early date. In the same year, 1219, as Pope Honorius authorised the founding of a new cathedral, King Henry granted to the bishop the right to hold a market, which in the revised scheme was sited a block north of that first main road. In the idea of devising a grid-plan there was nothing particularly new or original: there were plenty of Roman cities based on a grid, and in some, such as Winchester, the original pattern was carried over into later layouts.

What was distinctive about Salisbury's was that it was asymmetrical: partly because it was shaped by existing routes, including the earliest attempt at a by-pass – the diversion to the east of the route from Old Sarum to Harnham occasioned by the layout of the Close – and partly, by following the lie of the land, to aid the flow of the water along the watercourses. The division of the city into blocks allowed for further subdivision into standard rental units of 3 perches wide and 7

St Martin's Church. This etching is from Hall's ***Picturesque Memorials of Salisbury***, 1834. Referred to by Hall as St Martin in the Fields, it was until the 19th century at the heart of a separate enclave from the city proper, but referred to in the Middle Ages as St Martin's in Salisbury, indicating how far the bishop's manor of Salisbury extended. The church predates the cathedral and the other city parish churches, though it was largely rebuilt in the 15th century, with only the chancel readily identifiable as of the 13th century.

perches deep, a pattern observable in planned towns even before the Conquest, such as Cricklade in the north of Wiltshire, which, based on a single main street, has burgage plots mainly 2 perches wide and 12 deep.

At the other end of the scale, the city was divided into four wards: two between the Close and the road from Winchester to Wilton and a third to the south of these and east of the Close, which proved unsuitable for commercial exploitation, but was soon to be developed by the friars of the Franciscan order. The fourth – all that land to the north of the Winchester-Wilton road – may have been the common field for the ancient parish of St Martin. The immediate success of the first and second wards led to the exploitation of the fourth ward, and, early in the city's history, to the creation of a third new parish, St Edmund's. The division of the city into just three parishes is indicative of the grand scale of its conception, and contrasts markedly with Wilton, which at one time comprised as many as 12 parishes.

The streets themselves were a key feature of the design: wider than in many other towns of the time – wider, for example, than those of the Bastide St Louis, the new quarter of Carcassonne, laid out a generation later. It is perhaps to that design feature, capable of accepting types and densities of traffic never dreamt of by its founders, that the mediaeval city of Salisbury owes its survival to the present day. But the city owes its life and its vigour, despite the vicissitudes of later ages, to the cathedral, to which we now turn our attention.

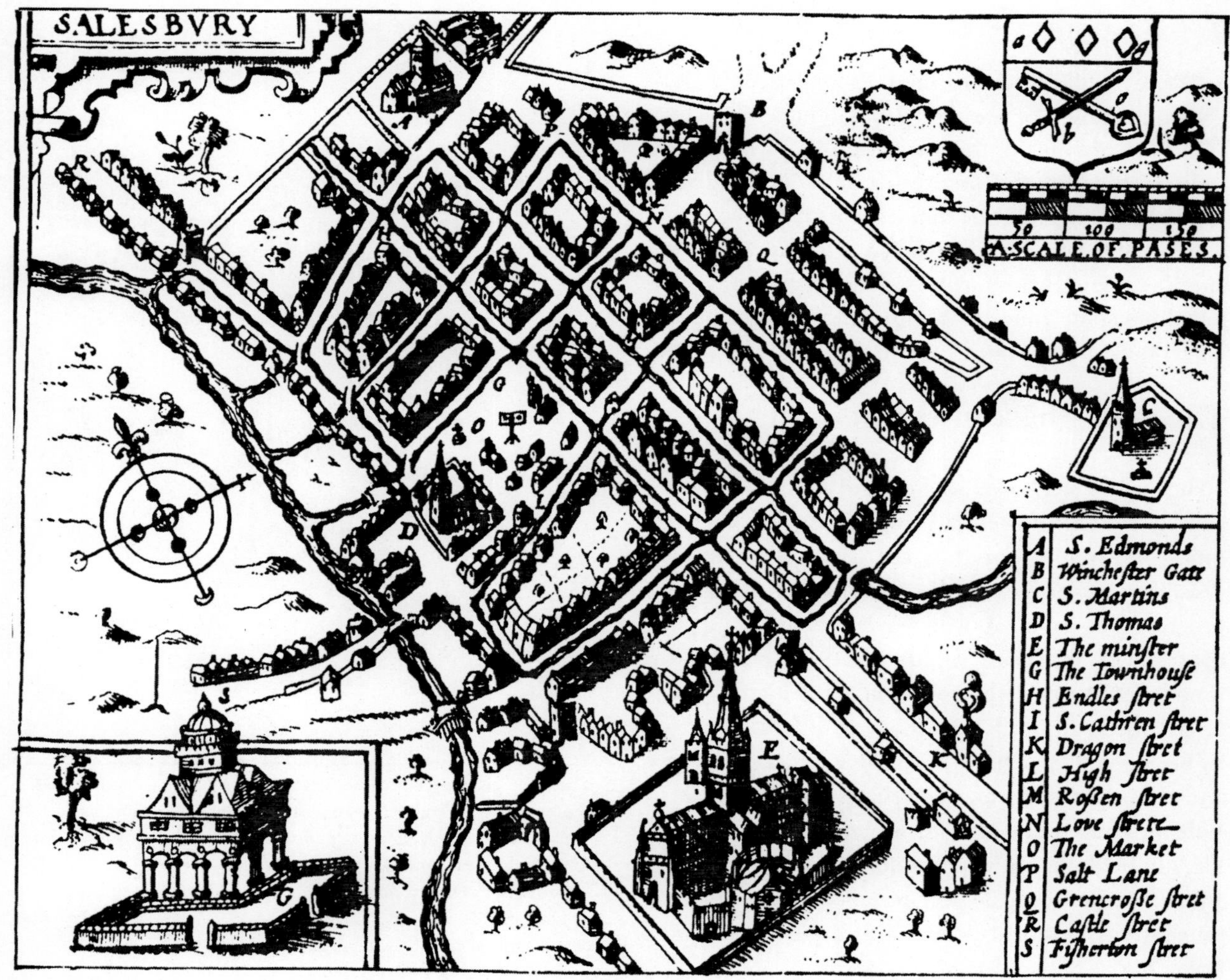

Speed's birds-eye view map of Salisbury. This shows the extreme northern limit of the town extending a little beyond the Castle Gate (upper left hand of picture), the thoroughfare west of St Thomas's (D on the map), while Minster Street, Butcher Row and Fish Row are relatively ill-defined. The bishop's guildhall and the Council House are just to the right of the pillory. The Friary is simply a large open space with St Martin's Church to the east.

Chapter 3

'Such singular and transcendent beauty'

The building of the new cathedral

SALISBURY Cathedral has long been held a paradigm of Early English Gothic architecture, on account of the purity and uniformity of its style, arising from the brief timescale of its building. In fact there are four distinct phases of its construction, of which the final phase and much else besides is now almost completely lost, owing to later restoration work. Our immediate concern is with the first three phases, which took place in about a century.

The First Phase of the Building

To begin with, we have seen how a decision to move the church and the chapter had long lain on the table, and much preparatory work had already been undertaken: thus, once permission had been granted for its building, progress was rapid. A wooden chapel was built and consecrated on Trinity Sunday, 1219. Stones for the foundation of the cathedral were laid at a great public ceremony on 28 April 1220, the feast of St Vitalis: three by Bishop Poore, on his own behalf and that of the Pope and the Archbishop of Canterbury, and one each by William Longespee, Earl of Salisbury, and his countess, Ela. Although the entire groundplan was determined in advance – for archaeological evidence suggests that the foundations were laid down all of a piece – the walls began to rise at the east end.

The three eastern chapels, consecrated in October 1225. At the left is the chapel of St Peter and the Apostles, in the centre the chapel of the Holy Trinity and All Saints, popularly known as the Lady Chapel, and to the right the chapel of St Stephen and the Martyrs. The illustration is from ***Price's Observations on ... the Cathedral***, 1753, and shows the original mediaeval roofs, which Price, as clerk of works at the cathedral, rebuilt in 1736.

By October 1225, three chapels were ready to be consecrated: the Lady Chapel, dedicated to the Holy Trinity and All Saints; to its south, the chapel of St Stephen and the martyrs; and to its north the chapel of St Peter and the apostles. The next year, the tombs of the three great bishops of Salisbury, Osmund, Roger and

Bishop Richard Poore. This statue faces into the main south transept of the cathedral and was donated in his memory and that of a later member of the Poore family who died in 1938. It is slightly anachronistic in that the bishop's model of the cathedral has a tower and spire, which is not known to have been part of Poore's original concept.

Jocelyn, were brought down from the old cathedral to the new, and the Earl of Salisbury was laid to rest there. Shortly afterwards, the account of the building by William de Waude, dean of the cathedral from 1220 to *c.*1236, finishes: for the ensuing history there is the evidence of entries in the Close Rolls and the account of Matthew Paris. Yet just over 30 years later, in 1258, Bishop Giles de Bridport consecrated the cathedral in the presence of the king, Henry III. By then the work outstanding amounted primarily to the building of the cloisters and the chapter house. A marginal note in a manuscript of the Statutes of Bishop Roger de Martival records that the church was completed on the Thursday in Holy Week, 25 March 1266, at a cost of 42,000 marks, or £28,000; on a par with the rebuilding costs of Westminster Abbey at about the same time.

Tomb slabs of Bishops Roger and Jocelyn. In 1226 the bodies of Salisbury's three great early bishops, Osmund, Roger of Caen and Jocelyn, were brought down from Old Sarum and reburied in the new cathedral, in shrines resplendent in jewels and gold-leaf. These did not survive the Reformation and it is recorded that it took 52 man-days to dismantle them in 1539.

Edmund Rich, treasurer of the cathedral, here portrayed as at the time of his death as Archbishop of Canterbury on his way to meet the Pope. The statuette is at Pontigny Abbey, where the saint is buried.

The Appeal for the Building

The sheer speed of the enterprise raises questions – of finance and of logistics. The cost of the building was met by the response to appeals, with charity beginning at home. Both the bishop and his capitular officers were landowners of substance, and they, together with the canons, contributed significantly to the costs of the building project. Indeed the canons were in effect taxed on their prebendal incomes: at the meeting of the chapter on 15 August – the Feast of the Assumption – 1220, it was decreed that delay or refusal to contribute would result in the seizure of produce from their estates. In addition, the canons travelled far and wide – even as far as Ireland – to raise money by preaching, gathering alms, and even, it would seem, to secure raw materials. Recent dendrochronological research has revealed that some of the oak used in the cathedral was Irish. Pledges were made by both clergy and laity when the stones were laid at the founding ceremony.

Other means of fund-raising among the laity included endowing a chantry, wherein a priest would offer prayers for the donor's soul, or by granting indulgences – remissions of the time spent in purgatory. The one campaign which would undoubtedly have lent weight to the appeal would have been the canonisation of Bishop Osmund: instigated some time around 1180, but destined to succeed only in 1457 after a second campaign. (Edmund Rich, treasurer of the cathedral at this time and Thomas Becket, both Archbishops of Canterbury, were canonised within a few years of their deaths). Substantial gifts were made in kind, ranging from the vast quantity – 12 years' supply – of Purbeck marble (in reality a hard, fossiliferous limestone) from the mines at Downshay, given by Alice Briwere, to the oak for the roof timbers from the royal forests, throughout Wiltshire and beyond. In addition, Henry III, renowned for his endowments to the Church and thus for the flowering of Early English Gothic architecture, granted the income from two of his manors to the building project.

Architects and Builders

The man responsible for the building of the cathedral was Elias of Dereham. He is referred to variously as

Elias of Dereham. Elias, as depicted in the statue facing into the main south transept of the cathedral, and donated by the Freemasons in 1946. Elias's most celebrated commission hitherto, which led him to be chosen for the work of designing Salisbury Cathedral and city, was the shrine of St Thomas at Canterbury.

'***mirabilis artifex***' or '***incomparabilis artifex***' – the admirable, or incomparable, craftsman – for his work on St Thomas Becket's shrine in Canterbury Cathedral, and he was probably the genius behind the overall design of the cathedral. However, his brief would also have included financial and commissioning responsibilities, arising from the exceptionally high level of trust accorded to him in legal and monetary matters. Stephen Langton, Archbishop of Canterbury, spoke of him as the only honest man in England, and he was variously an executor for three archbishops, and responsible for the distribution of most of the copies of the Magna Carta. He was probably responsible, alongside the treasurer, Edmund Rich, for the fundraising campaign and for securing the supplies of the building stone from the quarries at Tisbury and Purbeck. His key role in deter-

St Edmund of Abingdon: tomb at Pontigny Abbey. Following his career as treasurer at Salisbury Cathedral, St Edmund was appointed Archbishop of Canterbury, being consecrated in April 1234. While on his way to Rome to meet the Pope, St Edmund died at Soisy in November 1240, and was buried at the nearby Abbey of Pontigny, in Burgundy. His mortal remains are in a tomb above and behind the high altar, while a little statue of him is in an anteroom adjacent to the narthex at the abbey's west end.

mining the appearance of the cathedral is borne out by his career elsewhere, moving from diocese to diocese throughout the first half of the 13th century, and always when major building projects were in hand. As a prebendary at Wells Cathedral, built shortly before Salisbury, he knew Adam Locke, the master mason, and unsurprisingly his associates at Salisbury hailed as he did from East Anglia.

John Leland refers to Robert of Ely as chief mason, and cathedral records include the name of Nicholas of Ely, as '*cementarius*' – a mason or a builder. While it has been suggested that these are in fact one and the same person, Matthew Paris speaks of builders, in the plural, called from afar to design and build the new cathedral. Whatever their role in realising the grand design, the master masons would have been responsible for directing the building and for the decorative work. While much of the stonework would have been roughly fashioned at the quarries by the banker masons, it fell to bands of masons locally to assemble the dressed pieces. These, the most skilled craftsmen, comprised itinerant companies, engaged on a contract basis, who set up their quarters, referred to as lodges, where their work was: they were thus among the sources of inspiration for modern freemasonry. Legend has it that at one point they went on strike for an increase in their daily wage from a penny to a penny-farthing: when the city street-plan was worked out, the street which ran where the masons' encampment had been was named Pennyfarthing Street.

At the spot chosen for the cathedral, foundations were dug down to the flinty river gravel deposited in the Avon flood plain. This lies only four or five feet below ground level, and that is the approximate depth of the rammed-mortared foundations on which the cathedral rests. How could such a mass lie on

MAGNA CARTA OF 1215

SALISBURY CATHEDRAL

Salisbury Magna Carta. One of the six copies with which Elias of Dereham had been entrusted in July 1215, by which time the king and the barons were drifting back into a state of conflict.

foundations so shallow for the greater part of a millennium and not collapse? The answer is that the valley gravel within the crook of the Avon – and only there – is some 27ft deep, of a uniform consistency and, almost always waterlogged, is remarkably stable: in effect this is the cathedral's foundations. The building stones for the cathedral were both local limestones: the main source being the Tisbury quarries, 15 miles up the Nadder valley. While ease of access for both this and the Purbeck marble will have contributed substantially to the smooth progress and short timescale for the building, it undoubtedly guaranteed the unique appearance of the cathedral: not merely the uniformity of the building style, but the austere beauty of the greenish-grey hue to which its Tisbury stone weathers.

The Expression of an Idea

On account of its stylistic unity, the cathedral has long been acclaimed as a summation of Early English Gothic

The cathedral – a general view from the north-east, dating from 1747 and published in Price's ***Observations*** of 1753 includes a perspective ground-plan, and thus graphically demonstrates the numerical ratios underlying the cathedral's basic design.

architecture. In fact, the date of its commencement places it at one remove from its immediate antecedents such as Wells Cathedral, the choir of Canterbury Cathedral and St Hugh's choir at Lincoln Cathedral. Yet the later phase of Early English architecture, which includes the choirs at Worcester and Ely, the transepts at York, and the Nine Altars of Durham, and finds its peak in the Angel Choir and the Chapter House at Lincoln, represents a development of the style beyond Salisbury. In many ways Salisbury has more in common with French cathedral building of the period, from Chartres to Amiens by way of Tours, Rouen, Soissons and Le Mans. What sets Salisbury apart from its French contemporaries is the combination of simple decoration and relatively low elevation with a square-ended and quite complex ground-plan. In England, apart from St Thomas's shrine at Canterbury Cathedral, the hand of Elias is in all probability to be seen in the Great Hall of the archbishop's palace there, the Great Hall in Winchester Castle and the chapel at Lambeth Palace.

The reason, perhaps, why Salisbury has something of a transitional character, is that it was seen as the heir to the cathedral at Old Sarum, and even though it was built on a virgin site a spiritual continuity was being expressed in its design. At the same time the liturgical inheritance of the Use of Sarum and the need for the cathedral to function as a stage set for the great ceremonies of the Church's year explain the great size of both the choir and the nave, and indeed the prominence given in the design to the north porch, which faced the

Views of the Great Hall, Winchester. While at Salisbury, Elias enjoyed close relations with Peter des Roches, Bishop of Winchester, and with Henry III, and, as almost certainly the architect of Archbishop Walter's Great Hall at Canterbury, was the obvious candidate for the design of the king's Great Hall at Winchester.

city, and the cloisters. The cathedral's monumental scale, the grandeur of its isolation within the Close, the stress on harmony rather than decoration and the choice of building stones and grisaille glass all serve to represent a theological ideal. It reflects the desire of its founder, Bishop Poore, to create an architectural expression of the New Universal Church conveyed in the teachings prevalent in early 13th-century Paris, and promulgated in the canons of the fourth Lateran Council of 1215 and his own revision of the Use of Sarum.

Differences Over Time: the Tower and Spire

Between the cathedral as it was consecrated in 1258 and what we now have there are five major differences. Firstly, the crossing tower projected scarcely above the roof apexes. It may have had a low pyramidal roof or a

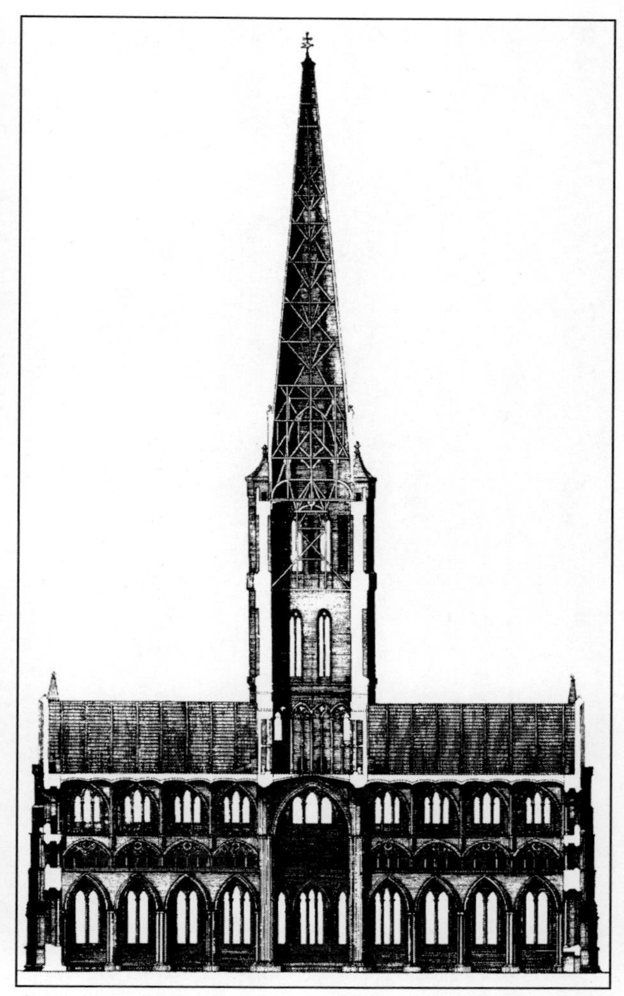

Cross-sectional diagram of the cathedral, from Price's ***Observations*** of 1753, which again demonstrates how the tower and spire were designed by reference to mathematical ratios similar to those informing the relationship between the ground-plan and elevation of the cathedral before the spire was built.

lead-covered spire; but there was certainly no need for the tower to project above the roofs as does Winchester's, because Salisbury, like Chichester and present-day Chester, had a freestanding campanile with a spire projecting some 200ft. Standing to the north of the cathedral, between it and the city, the campanile with its ring of 10 bells was, like the cathedral's north façade, part of the face it presented to the world outside. This meant that when the present tower and spire were built, early in the 13th century, they could be designed by reference purely to the arithmetical ratios which had informed the configuration of the cathedral itself. Not having to withstand the lateral stresses imposed by swinging bells gave its unknown architect the freedom

The Bell Tower. The belfry stood to the north of the cathedral, whence the sound of its bells would have been heard throughout the city. By the time this engraving was made in 1843, the belfry was no more than a memory; based on a drawing by John Buckler, it shows the belfry with the low pyramidal roof which replaced the spire in 1768.

Inverted arches. These arches were built across the eastern transepts to assist with bearing the lateral thrust on the eastern end of the building, imposed by the additional weight of the tower and spire.

to dare to build a tower that extended to 220ft from the ground, and a spire which extended a further 180ft.

Even so, the tower had to be reinforced with iron bracing and buttressing, internally and externally, for the tower and spire together have been estimated to weigh 6,500 tons. Indeed, the lateral forces on the rest of the building were such that inverted arches had to be inserted at the eastern transepts, and, later, the nave had to be buttressed externally. When the tower and spire were built has, in the absence of written record, been the subject of scholarly debate; but the quantity and type of decoration, known as 'ball-flower' places the tower in the second decade of the 14th century, and other architectural associations prompt even earlier estimates.

The moving force behind the project must have been bishops Roger de Martival and Simon of Ghent. Certainly, the lack of reference to the tower and spire in

Ball-flower decoration on the tower and spire. This is visible close at hand on the Cathedral Tower tours, but otherwise most forcibly in this engraving by Le Keux, illustrating John Britton's ***History and antiquities of the Cathedral Church of Salisbury***, 1814, which is one of the main reasons for ascribing the building of the tower and spire to the episcopates of Roger de Martival and Simon of Ghent in the early 14th century.

Pillars buckling under the weight of the tower. The engineering limits of the building can be seen from this picture showing the effect of the weight of the tower and spire on the crossing pillars.

Two brass plates in the floor of the crossing date from Naish's and Price's surveys of the early 19th century. The diagonal line is part of the octagonal outline of the spire's cross-section and shows how far out of true the tower and the spire are.

the Chapter Act Books (which provide a record from 1331 onwards) indicates that the building was probably finished by the early 1330s. At 404ft the spire is the tallest in the British Isles, and among Europe's mediaeval spires it yields place only to Strasbourg. At the time of its building, however, this was not the case: Lincoln and Old St Paul's cathedrals had spires some 50ft higher, although these had collapsed by the mid-16th century. However, the builders at Salisbury took the revolutionary step, for a spire on that scale, of building it in stone, and it was on that bold decision that the spire's survival probably depended. The spire's

Strainer arches. A solution to the problem of stresses imposed by the tower and spire was attempted in the 15th century with the installation of these strainer arches across the main transepts. Only on later investigations was it learned that one of the strainer arches was free of the piers it was intended to support.

security has been an object of concern throughout its almost 700-year history. A glance up the Purbeck marble shafts of the crossing demonstrates graphically the stresses imposed by the additional weight of the tower and spire, and strainer arches were installed across the transepts in the 15th century to strengthen the crossing. However, by then the structure had settled and was stable: a later survey revealed that one of the strainer arches was having no effect. Wren's survey of 1668 revealed that the spire leant nearly 30 inches out of true, and a start was made on external buttressing, but Price's survey of 1736 revealed no further deterioration, and with a continuing programme of maintenance it is still with us today. Despite its location in the river valley, it is visible, in Aubrey's words, like a fine Spanish needle, from 16 miles away. Not so the belfry, which was demolished in 1791 as part of the rationalisation of the appearance of the cathedral precincts under the general direction of James Wyatt.

Differences Over Time: the Glazing, Ancillary Buildings and the West Front

The third major difference is in the glazing of the cathedral windows. While not so large a part of the design as in decorated or perpendicular Gothic architecture, the type of glazing at once determines the atmosphere in an Early English church. In Salisbury, grisaille glass, so called because it is coloured in varying shades of silver and grey, was used extensively; principally, it is believed, in the nave and choir aisles. Coloured glass, perhaps within a grisaille setting, would have been used only above the altars. The impact on the interior lighting of the cathedral would have been dramatically different from that of the predominantly blue glazing at Chartres, for example, and thus quite different from the effect produced by the Prisoners of Conscience windows. The relatively clear light would have revealed the paintings on the vaulting of the choir and eastern transept, and the colouring of the mouldings on the tombs, the pulpitum and the vaulting generally. The effect can be seen in the windows of the transepts at York Minster, glazed in grisaille from about 1240 onwards: some of the glass survives in the south-east transept, while other glass, much of it originally from the Chapter House, has been reassembled in a window in the north chancel aisle. The decorated glass can be seen in the south nave aisle, again incorporating

Glass at St Leonard's, Grateley. This glass, removed from St Stephen's chapel, on the south side of the east end of the cathedral, shows the martyrdom of St Stephen, and it dates from the 13th century.

Bird's-eye view of the Chapter House from cathedral. An etching of the cathedral's main ancillary buildings, the cloisters, library and chapter house, by C. Castle, from Hall's ***Picturesque Memorials***, 1834.

Chapter House fragments, and depicting the Tree of Jesse; a little more survives in a window in the nearby parish church of St Leonard, Grateley. At Salisbury, the glazing, subtly transmuting the pure northern light, would have been of a piece with the overall design philosophy.

Next, there are the cloisters and the Chapter House, without which the cathedral could not be considered complete. As originally planned the cloisters were rather smaller than we see them today, for there is evidence of the western wall having been moved outwards, and in 1263 the dean and chapter acquired part of the bishop's land to extend the cloister southwards. It is possible to see from the gradual shift in the design of the cloister roof bosses, how the building began with the north walk and proceeded clockwise, finishing with the west walk. Over time, the stylised depiction of foliage known as 'stiff-leaf' yields to a more naturalistic representation, and finally includes animals and people. The probable timescale for the building ranges from the 1250s to the 1260s, corresponding with the statement that the cathedral was finished in 1266. On stylistic grounds, the Chapter House dates from about the same period as the west walk of the cloisters. The discovery in the 19th century of pennies from the reign of Edward I in the Chapter House foundations has been adduced in support of a date of around 1280; that evidence is now open to question, and it seems unlikely that the Chapter House was built much, if at all, later than this. In many ways, with its abundance of figurative sculpture and its grisaille glazing, the Chapter House today, of all the cathedral buildings, most closely reflects its original appearance, even though it was comprehensively restored in the 19th century.

Finally, the one great exception to the cathedral's triumph of form over ornamentation is the west front, presenting a veritable gallery of the company of saints and of major personalities in the cathedral's history. Yet although there were over 200 niches available for statuary, it seems that none were occupied when the cathedral was consecrated, and the task of populating them proceeded slowly with the passage of time. The presence of statues in the original scheme can be inferred from surviving mediaeval securing loops, and more tellingly from the numbers of corbel busts in the arcading (once described, with those elsewhere in the cathedral, as a '13th-century picture gallery'); yet an engraving of 1836 shows the west front all but bereft of statuary. The surviving mediaeval sculptures date from the later 13th century: the serried ranks we see today almost all date from Sir George Gilbert Scott's restoration of the 1860s and 1870s.

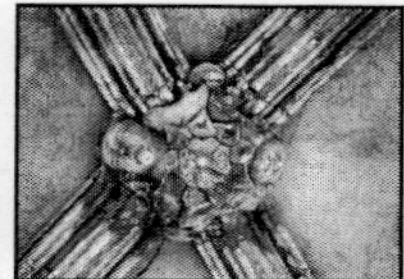

Roof-bosses in the cloisters. The subtle stylistic gradation of the cloister roof-bosses, clockwise from the west end of the north walk, is key evidence for the building sequence of the cloister walks and can be traced from 'stiff-leaf' foliage (left), through more naturalistic representation (centre), and finally to animals and people (right), along the west walk.

There were thus two quite distinct building campaigns, either side of the consecration in 1258. The most likely explanation is that at his accession in 1256, Bishop Giles de Bridport deemed the work far enough advanced to fix a date for the consecration, in compliance with a statute of 1237 which decreed the consecration within two years of any church whose walls were built.

The carvings in the Chapter House have suffered despoliation during periods of religious intolerance, but were thoroughly restored in the 19th century. The sequence depicts scenes from the Old Testament, starting with the Creation and finishing with the journey to the Promised Land. Top left: Noah's Ark; top right: Moses sees the Lord in the burning bush, and the Israelites cross the divided waters of the Red Sea, which then close in upon Pharaoh's army; above: Moses strikes the rock from which water springs; Moses receives the Ten Commandments on tablets of stone.

Thus, even without cloisters and chapter house, the cathedral had to be consecrated when it was. The ensuing timespan for the subsequent building campaign can be put down to money, or the lack of it, evinced by such fundraising measures during the 1270s as the granting of indulgences in return for contributions to the building fund, and gaining the right to hold a second fair during the Feast of St Remigius, in October of each year.

The relatively minor changes to the fabric of the cathedral over the ensuing centuries (which include the construction of the Hungerford and Beauchamp Chantries, the despoliation during the Reformation and Wyatt's and later restorations) arise from the city's changing circumstances, and are thus more appropriately considered within those contexts. It is to the life of the city that we must now turn our attention.

Chapter 4
The Early Years of the City

THE irony of Salisbury's history was that during its heyday – its halcyon years as a centre of trade and industry until around 1500 – its economic pre-eminence went hand-in-hand with political and fiscal subjugation to its bishops. By the time this relationship was severed and the city fathers were able to take control of their own destiny, about a century after the Reformation, the opportunity to capitalise on the city's textile trade had long since passed with the decline in Southampton's fortunes, and the rise of other ports, such as London and Bristol, which favoured the development of other local centres of industry. How this came to pass is the subject of this chapter. When we left Salisbury, it was as Elias de Dereham's grand design. Just as we can date the birth of the cathedral to 28 April 1220, so we can date the birth of the city with equal precision to 30 January 1227, when Henry III granted the first full charter.

The Infant City

The rights granted to the people of Salisbury furnish us with a portrait of an already flourishing urban community, functioning as an important market centre. The citizens were granted freedom from a range of royal feudal dues – toll, pontage, passage, pedage, lestage, stallage, carriage and other duties. Pontage was a bridge-toll, levied for its maintenance; lestage, or lastage, was a duty on goods sold in markets by the last – a measure used for a variety of goods ranging from fish and grain to textiles and hides. Stallage and carriage were imposed on market traders for, respectively, setting up their stalls and conveying their goods by wheeled transport.

Thus Salisbury was liberated from the constraints of the feudal system; or rather the power to levy taxes was placed in the bishop's hands, but the immunity otherwise from such a wide range of dues gave to the new city unparalleled opportunities for development. Merchants coming into the city were to enjoy free access to the city, 'so that they pay the customs that are just and due'. The right to hold a market every Tuesday was granted, as was that of a fair for 10 days at the feast of the Assumption. Not for nothing was Salisbury ordained 'a free city for ever', and, moreover, another clause in the charter conferred 'all the other liberties and immunities which our Citizens of Winchester enjoy'. So much for the economy: also included in the charter were the rights to fortify the city and to alter roads and bridges providing access to the city, which imply, even at this early date, a broadening of the scope of the venture.

However, perhaps the most important aspect of the founding charter is that the key rights and powers are vested in the person of the bishop. Nowhere in the 1227 charter is there any mention of how the city was to organise its affairs, nor of the relationship between the leading citizens and the bishop and his officers; but a hint is given in the clause prohibiting the citizens from conveying their property either to a church or a religious community. The fact, moreover, that Salisbury is described as a free city also implies the existence of a Guild Merchant, both an association of the tradespeople and the city's electorate for officers to direct its affairs.

The Potential for Growth and the Chequers

Doubtless it was initially the case that the citizens welcomed the unique opportunity to prosper and develop under episcopal patronage and guardianship. The plan of the city, comprising a grid of six streets running east-west and five running north-south, offered the potential for more than 20 blocks for development. In fact, even though one was almost completely given over to the market, there remain 21

Map of the city showing the Chequers. This map, published in 1797 by Donn, shows Salisbury with little more extensive development than there had been three or four hundred years before. It names 20 of the 21 Chequers, and also shows the extent to which the environs beyond were still cultivated as gardens.

blocks, known as the Chequers. Though the standard plot, on which an annual ground-rent of one shilling was payable in half-yearly instalments, was three perches (16½ yards) by 7 perches (38½ yards), it could be subdivided and sub-let, and plots on prime sites, such as at corners, or facing the market, often were. Examination of the Ordnance Survey and other large-scale plans of the 19th century shows this process at work, before being reversed by the modern trend for plots to be combined to accommodate larger single developments. Away from the hubbub of the market, change of both sorts has been less, and, as at Cricklade, in the north of the county, it is still possible to discern some of the original burgages.

The Chequers have distinctive names, which reflect two aspects of Salisbury's early importance as a market centre. There are those named after inns, some of which, like the White Horse and the White Hart, remain, and others, like the Antelope and the Blue Boar, the Cross Keys, the Three Swans and the Three Cups, which have disappeared, the former two long since, the latter three almost within living memory. The names of the Three Cups and the Cross Keys are preserved in modern developments: a range of courtyard apartments in the former instance, and a shopping precinct in the latter. Other Chequers are named after prominent tenants, men like William Swayne, who in Bishop Beauchamp's rental list of 1455 is shown as having more than 20 properties.

The Market and Trades

At the heart of the city lay the market, and the names of some of the streets which face onto the market, and others lying directly behind the present market square, indicate the range of goods sold and activities undertaken: Oatmeal Row, Butcher Row, Silver Street, Fish Row and Ox Row. At the junction of the first three of these is the Poultry Cross, the last survivor of Salisbury's four market crosses, of which three were in the main market square. There was a cheese cross near the junction of Blue Boar Row and Castle Street, and a wool cross at the other end of Blue Boar Row. The fourth cross, Barnard's Cross, was at the junction of Culver Street and Barnard Street, in the south-eastern outskirts of the city, and was the focus for the trade in livestock. Originally, the entire space between Blue Boar Row and the New Canal, and from Queen Street westwards as far as Castle Street and the High Street, was devoted to the Market Place: almost an acre, and at least double the present area of the market. Such an area was by no means out of the ordinary: in Yorkshire, Richmond's market place is Britain's largest, and is about three acres.

Poultry Cross. One of four market crosses in Salisbury, the Poultry Cross was also where vegetables were sold.

What has happened, meanwhile, in Salisbury, is a process of encroachment: in areas occupied by, for example, the butchers and the fishmongers, temporary stalls have been replaced by permanent structures. That this was happening at an early stage can be seen in the 1455 rental list, which refers to properties in Minster Street, Butcher Row and the place of the fishmongers' stalls. The earliest encroachment, however, was the city's first new parish church. Its dedication to St Thomas was perhaps to be expected, given not only the popularity of the saint's cult since his canonisation in 1173, but also, more especially, Elias of Dereham's close association with the design of his shrine at Canterbury, and the transfer of his remains thereto in 1220. A chapel of ease would have been built at about the time work was beginning on the cathedral; a quarter of a century later, in 1248, there is reference to St Thomas's as a parish church. The consecration in 1269 of the third and last of Salisbury's mediaeval parish churches, St Edmund's, marks the limit of the northern expansion of the city. As with St Thomas's, the new church was dedicated to a saint only recently canonised, and one with a strong

The inscription on the central pillar details the Poultry Cross's history.

local connection, for St Edmund of Abingdon had been, from 1222 to 1234, Edmund Rich, the treasurer to the cathedral.

The streets beyond the Market Place, as well as those in and around the Market Place, point up the importance of trade. Catherine Street's name is a corruption of ***carterne*** – the street of the carters, while Chipper Lane was derived from a personal name – but that, in turn, was derived from a trade (chippers, or chapmen, being retail traders or market men), while certain areas around the Market Place were known respectively as Ironmonger, Cordwainer, Wheeler and Smiths' Row, and somewhere along Silver Street or the High Street lay ***le Cokerewe***, the cooks' row.

Salisbury's early success as a market centre can be gauged from the evidence of complaints from the neighbouring market towns of Old Sarum and Wilton. As early as 1240, the elders of Wilton protested that in Salisbury markets were being held every day of the week, contrary to their charter entitlement, and the complaint was reiterated in a dispute in 1274, when it was claimed that Old Sarum and other neighbouring

This 19th-century market day engraving captures the busy nature of market days down the centuries.

St Thomas's Church. Originally a chapel-of-ease for the cathedral, St Thomas's became the first parish church of the new city, dedicated to the recently-canonized Archbishop of Canterbury, Thomas Becket, who became the object of a cult following his assassination in 1172.

St Edmund's Church. As the city expanded the need for a second new parish was met by this church, originally at least double its present length, and served by a college of resident clergy. It was founded in 1269 by Bishop Walter de la Wyle. Like St Thomas's it was dedicated to a recently-deceased and greatly revered Archbishop of Canterbury, Edmund Rich, who had been treasurer at the cathedral in its earliest years.

market towns were affected, not just Wilton. Whatever the substance of these grievances, they have, as we have noted in Wilton's case, as much to do with their decline as Salisbury's success. The eventual compromise, in 1315, permitted a second market day every Saturday, and this dispensation, of markets on Tuesday and Saturday, remains to this day. Even Winchester, at one time the royal capital of England, had suffered as a consequence of its political importance, having undergone siege in the reigns of Stephen and John. By 1228, when Salisbury was still at an early stage of development, Winchester was described as being in a state of 'poverty and ruin', and it was the gap represented by Winchester's enfeeblement which Bishop Poore sought to exploit.

The Development of the City's Government

Against this background of a thriving market community under the bishop's tutelage there are sporadic early references which imply a system of government: state papers of 1249 refer to a mayor of Salisbury, and the names are known of a further dozen between 1261 and 1302. By 1249, also, there were established traditions of aldermen, and of burgesses – the property-holders – being also members of the Guild Merchant, and having thereby a political status and role in the city's affairs. A case from the Assize Roll of that year refers to one Robert of Alderbury securing his status as a freeman by proving that he had dwelt in Salisbury for 10 years, 'in scot and lot, and in the Merchant Guild as free burgess'. The office of reeve is known from 1265, and by 1298, and probably much earlier, the city had its own seal.

Our earliest evidence for the form of the city's governance, however, dates from 1306, when new statutes were granted. Ironically, these followed a long and bruising dispute between the leading citizens and the bishop over taxation, which the bishop, Simon of Ghent, won. When the dispute was heard before the king's council, the citizens were offered the choice of accepting the bishop's right to levy the tax in the future and retaining their liberties, or denying that right and foregoing their liberties. The citizens, represented by their mayor, Richard of Ludgershall, chose the second option, and within a year the city's economy was in

The bishop's guildhall. There are no known illustrations of the guildhall before it was demolished, and all extant representations are based on the watercolour made during its demolition in about 1790, now in the Salisbury and South Wiltshire Museum, or are imaginative reconstructions.

ruins. When the citizens were ready to come to terms, the resulting royal charter was drawn up by the city's leaders and Master Walter Hervey, Archdeacon of Salisbury.

The charter established, or more likely reasserted, such rights as that of electing a mayor, who then had to be presented to the bishop's steward or bailiff, and to discharge his office, as their junior. The same constraints applied to other civic officers. The bishop remitted those duties for which citizens had been liable during the dispute if they would submit to Hervey, and the existence of the Guild Merchant was confirmed, with membership conditional on submission to the bishop through Archdeacon Hervey. Among the prescriptions for the administration of the market, stallholders had to pay dues to the bishop before being allotted a pitch, and no meat or fish was to be sold before 6am except to the bishop and other residents of the Close, on pain of forfeiture to the bishop's court. The tangible reminder of episcopal power was the guildhall, probably built by Simon of Ghent, and in the same spot in the Market Place as the present guildhall. Although the city fathers had a hall of their own near St Thomas's Church, official and legal business of the kind referred to in the 1306 statutes would have been transacted in the bishop's guildhall, where there was also a gaol.

Throughout the Middle Ages and beyond, the bishop's power rankled. Occasionally, there were civil disturbances, and a dispute in 1395 echoed the events of 1305–6, while the promulgation of new statutes on a number of occasions represented the reassertion of the bishop's rights, but also concessions to the city, notably to hold property. As with other instances of political unrest throughout history, the granting of privileges to the disadvantaged served as a catalyst for more serious disputes. In 1450, at the time of Cade's rebellion, Bishop Ayscough was murdered by a gang led by a brewer from Salisbury, an outrage symptomatic of the general unrest, but at the same time bound up with local animosities.

A more characteristic dispute was that between William Swayne and John Hall in 1465 over a plot of land on which Swayne wished to build a house for his chantry priest. The plot was claimed by Swayne to have been in the bishop's gift, but by Hall to be the city's property. Hall, mayor 15 years before, and the leader of a petition to the king in 1453 for a charter of incorporation, was again called upon, as mayor, to present the city's case before the king, and the dispute broadened into conflicting claims for the city's independence and the continuation of the bishop's rights. Partly because of Hall's intransigence, and that of the city fathers (he was imprisoned for his behaviour to the king, but the city refused to elect a new mayor in his stead) and partly because of outside circumstances (the resumption of hostilities in the Wars of the Roses), the dispute dragged on until 1474, being finally resolved in the bishop's favour. As David Burnett has remarked, if Hall had been successful, the subsequent history of Salisbury might have been very different.

Wool – the Source of Salisbury's Wealth

Brought into the limelight by this dispute, the protagonists were typical of the entrepreneurial class whose efforts brought about Salisbury's meteoric rise in the first three centuries of its existence. Although, as we have seen, Salisbury's success was based on its symbiotic combination of cathedral city and market centre, the third ingredient, which propelled it from little more than a greenfield site to one of England's top 10 cities in scarcely more than a century, was wool. Initially, the trade was in raw wool, and Salisbury was placed neither better nor worse than any other market town surrounded by downland on which flocks of sheep were grazed and with ready access to ports like Southampton through which to export their produce. A taxation roll dating from 1332 detailing occupations shows that there were textile workers – a dyer, a napper and a shearer, for example, but there was no preponderance of such trades.

The catalyst, which propelled Salisbury from strength to strength, was the decision by Edward III to tax exports of raw wool through the mechanism of the Staple to finance his military campaigns in the Hundred Years' War, and the abundance of water-power in the neighbourhood which could be harnessed to drive mills to mechanise the fulling process, the heaviest and dirtiest stage in textile production. With the decline of the Flemish textile industry, all the ingredients were in place for Salisbury's to take off. The speciality was a medium-grade striped cloth called a ray, for which there was an extensive home market, mainly among better-off peasants, but also customers as diverse as liveried servants and prostitutes, who wore hoods of ray to advertise their calling, and, indeed, were ordered to do so in 1452 by the city, on pain of imprisonment.

From a handful of textile workers in 1332, the proportion of the city's tradesmen involved in the textile trade had increased to almost half by 1400, and also by this time, records show about ⅞ths of Wiltshire's textile production, counting in pieces, coming from Salisbury and its immediate environs. The production of textiles, exported through Southampton and other ports such as Christchurch, Lymington and Poole, found markets in the Baltic and the Low Countries, Portugal and the Mediterranean, and the returning imports added greatly to an already rich variety of goods produced and sold in the city.

Merchants and Trade

Apart from prerequisites for the cloth trade – the blue and red dyes woad and madder, and alum, used as a

The interior views are from Hall's ***Picturesque Memorials***, 1834 (top) and from a billboard of the later 19th century when the hall was home to Watson's, china and glass retailers.

John Hall. This portrait of Hall, resplendent in the formal attire of the period, is taken from an original in a stained-glass window.

fixative – imports included wines from Italy and France, of which in the early 15th century 25,000 gallons per year were traded in Salisbury. John Hall, four times Salisbury's mayor and three times its Member of Parliament, is the most celebrated of the city's merchant class in the 15th century. A measure of his wealth can be gauged from the fact that when, in 1444, the king imposed a levy of £40 on the city, Hall's contribution was 6s, or ¾ of one per cent; in 1449, the levy was £66, of which Hall's share was £1 6s 8d, or two per cent. His ship, the caravel ***James***, was berthed at Poole and used for the import of dyestuffs, almonds, fruit, salmon, herring, soap, tar and iron, and on occasion for piracy. Another merchant at the time imported a similar range of goods, and in addition, brushes, teazles, hemp, hats and steel nails.

As well as his ship, Hall had a shop known as the Doggehole, and the house on New Canal which bears his name, among his 16 properties recorded in the 1455 rental list. There are considerable numbers of city centre properties with associations with mediaeval merchants, of which there are two in Queen Street: No.9, William

House of John a Porte. Despite its popular name – based on a misreading of documentary evidence – this property actually belonged in the late 14th and early 15th century to two men called John Cammell. The first was a grocer, the second, like John Port in 1446, mayor of Salisbury, in 1449. To its left is William Russell's house, of similar antiquity despite its 18th-century frontage.

Russel's house; and No.8 next door, famously but erroneously associated with John Porte, who was mayor in 1446. The naming of several of the Chequers – Vanner's, Parson's, Gore's, Rolfe's and Swayne's – reflects substantial if not majority holdings of properties therein.

Mediaeval Piety

Investment in the hereafter has left equally tangible reminders: reference has already been made to Swayne's chantry priest: his chantry chapel can still be seen in St Thomas's Church, and the corresponding chapel to the north was built by William Ludlow, a prominent landowner in Blue Boar and Black Horse Chequers. Smaller but no less telling reminders of such associations are the shields on a capital carved with the (possible) merchants' marks of William Lightfoot and

Swayne's chapel, St Thomas's Church. William Swayne maintained this as a chantry, and his merchant's mark and arms can be seen on shields borne by angels on the roof timbers, as can an inscription exhorting the reader to pray for the souls of Swayne, his wife and his father. The housing of the chantry priest was the subject of a celebrated and long-running dispute between Swayne and John Hall.

The doom painting, St Thomas's Church. This is one of few survivors, depicting Christ in majesty admitting the souls arising from their graves at the left, and ascending to heaven, while those of the damned disappear into the maw of Hell at the right. From 1593 the painting was underneath whitewash; then it came to light and was restored/repainted in 1881. This artist's impression was published in 1843.

John Wyot, or the pillar inscribed with the name of the donor, John Nichol. The mediaeval view of man's place in the cosmos is powerfully portrayed in the doom painting above the chancel arch in St Thomas's. Belief in the efficacy of priestly intercession on one's behalf was not confined to any one class in mediaeval society, and the Swayne chapel had its counterparts in the cathedral, the Hungerford and Beauchamp chapels. These were built against the walls of the Lady Chapel: Robert, Lord Hungerford's, to the north, in 1471, and Bishop Richard Beauchamp's to the south, in 1481.

The Rise of the Craft Guilds

Although, as we have seen, a high proportion of the city's population was directly involved in the textile trade, it is symptomatic of the city's prosperity that there arose craft guilds. Established from a very early date to guard the interests of workers and traders in specific sectors and products, these had a broader membership than the Guild Merchant. By 1420, there were 19 such guilds, and they represented 36 different trades. Thus, the cloth trades – the weavers, fullers, tailors and dyers each had their own guilds, as did others whose members were numerous, such as the innkeepers, bakers, butchers, skinners and tanners. Others grouped together had interests in common, such as the shoemakers and curriers (leather dressers), the goldsmiths, blacksmiths and brasiers, and the bookbinders, parchment makers and glovers, who all dealt

The Giant and Hob-Nob. The giant represented St Christopher, the patron saint of the Tailors' Guild, and Hob-Nob his hobby-horse. The pair featured in processions and other celebrations until they were retired to the Museum in 1869, being brought out on special occasions, the last being 1977, for the Queen's Silver Jubilee and 750th anniversary of the founding of the city.

John Wynchestre's house, left to Trinity Hospital in 1458. In more recent years the property housed a shoe shop and the local branch of Thornton's, chocolatiers, and is presently occupied by a dispensary for traditional Chinese medicine.

with fine leather. Other guilds were made up of somewhat more disparate interests: the Joiners' Guild included carpenters, masons, tilers, and bowmakers, fletchers and coopers.

Just as the Guild Merchant was central to the administration of the city, so the craft guilds were inextricably bound up with the life of the city in several ways. Perhaps the most spectacular were the pageants, held on major feast days such as St George's and St John the Baptist's, St Osmund's and St Peter's. On these occasions a great procession would be led by the mayor and the corporation, all on horseback, preceded by torchbearers, armed retainers, the banner of the Guild of St George (the Guild Merchant), trumpeters and the other traditional musicians known as waits, and the effigy of St George. This cavalcade would be followed by all the guilds in turn, starting with the tailors, bearing a giant effigy of St Christopher, accompanied by a swordbearer, a mace-bearer, Morris dancers and Hob-Nob, the hobby-horse still, like the Giant, to be seen in the Salisbury and South Wiltshire Museum. Processions like these would also be held to welcome royalty, as happened when Henry VII and his queen, Elizabeth of York, came to Clarendon in 1496.

The guilds might also be called upon to assist with more serious demands of state, as when, in 1415, they were required to contribute towards the armed forces and the levy of 100 marks imposed by King Henry V on his way to France, shortly before Agincourt, and again in 1474, when Edward IV demanded of the city a contingent for his expeditionary force against France, when the city ledger lists the requirement, guild by guild. Because the Avon was at this time navigable as far as Christchurch, Salisbury was technically a seaport,

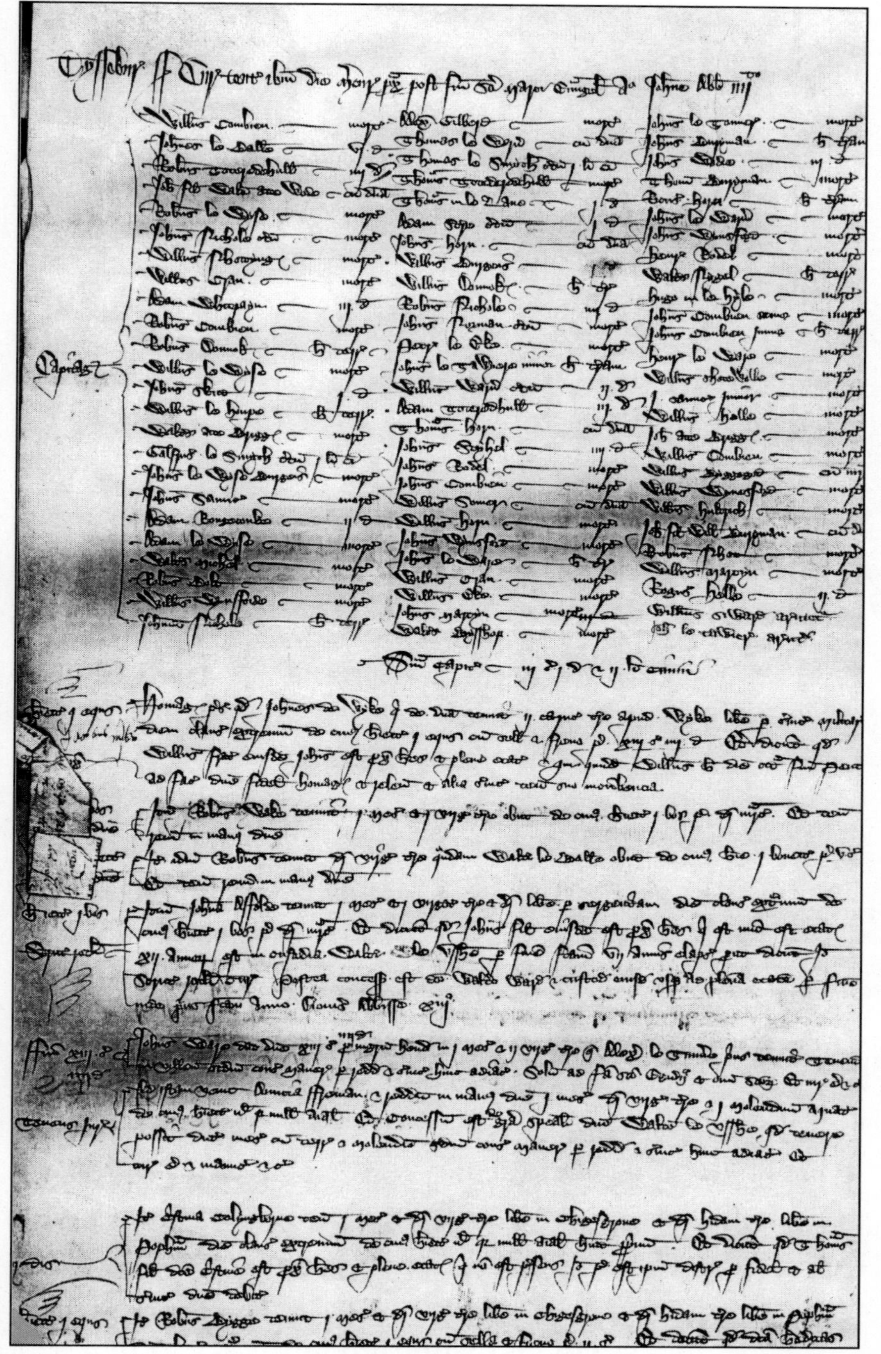

Tisbury Rent Roll, 1346. It lists tenants' names, and the sums they paid in rent – or else the abbreviation for mortuus – dead.

were ordered to take part in their construction. Like the great merchants such as Hall, Swayne and Webb, members of the craft guilds acquired great wealth, and like them, they had due regard for their souls and those of their loved ones in the hereafter. They included men like John Wynchestre, a barber, who left his house, on the corner of Minster and Silver Streets, to the master and brethren of Trinity Hospital to pray for their souls and distribute alms to the poor.

Salisbury's Growth and the Origins of its Decline

However, if Salisbury's wealth was built on the textile trade, it was, arguably, maintained by its role as a market centre and the range of other trades. Within two centuries of the city's foundation its population was about 5,000, the seventh largest English city. The first century of Salisbury's life was a time of rising population and migration into towns: in Salisbury's case early tax records provide evidence of such immigration, with many surnames derived from local placenames. But the second century was a time of economic recession, exacerbated by the Black Death. While we have no statistics for the plague's impact on Salisbury, the city is unlikely to have escaped, and the sheer horror of the epidemic is readily conveyed by a contemporary rent roll from Tisbury, a dozen miles up the Nadder valley, listing 76 tenants, of whom 42 are dead.

Yet still Salisbury bucked the trend. By 1503, Salisbury was ninth in a list of towns compiled for a

and was thus liable to be called upon to assist in the naval defence of the realm. During Henry VI's reign, the city built and manned the *Trout*, which was employed in defending the coast of Kent. Similarly, when the city's defences – the gates, bars and earth ramparts – were called into question in the reign of Henry V, the guilds

City Council House. Begun in 1579 and finished in 1584, the old Council House stood directly in front of the present Guildhall. Serious damage by fire in 1780 was one factor prompting the decision to replace it with the present guildhall.

royal assessment, behind London, Bristol, York, Lincoln, Gloucester, Norwich, Shrewsbury and Oxford. Its population, which was to decline slightly throughout the century, was about 8,000. But then, at least as regards its economy, the city bucked the national trend the other way. The causes were fourfold, but in the main they resulted from Salisbury's clothiers' inability to react to changing circumstances.

Firstly, there was a change in fashion, with demand rising for undyed broadcloth, to which Salisbury's merchants did not respond until the market had been well established elsewhere. This slowness of response may have been caused by the fragmentation of the processes of production, all in the hands of different independent producers. The demand for broadcloth favoured new systems of economic organisation, in which the clothiers had far tighter control on all stages of manufacture. Next, import duties on woad depressed trade. Finally, Southampton declined as the London Staple grew in power and tightened its grip on the cloth export trade. Some merchants established trading links with London, but the last of Salisbury's merchants trading through Southampton during the 1570s went bankrupt.

The Reformation and the Council's Growing Powers

These vicissitudes took place against the background of the greatest social upheaval in Salisbury's short history since the Black Death; namely, the Reformation. One result of the Reformation was the secularisation of the craft guilds, which had been among the major sponsors of the chantries – the endowments of priests to pray for the souls of the departed – of which there were 10 in Salisbury. In fact, it was the range of their secular activities that spared the guilds from being suppressed; nevertheless they sustained heavy losses of plate and other movable wealth, and the despoliation of chapels they had endowed. The other consequence of the Reformation was that the monarch became head of the church, and that may ultimately have been to the advantage of the city fathers in their quest for freedom through a fresh charter of incorporation.

The powers of the mayor and the council had gradually increased during the decades following the Reformation, as the episcopacy had been occupied increasingly with spiritual and doctrinal concerns. Thus, in 1562, Anthony Weekes was appointed to clean the streets, at an annual salary of £20: to clear away 'all such myre, durt, dust and soyle'. This included rubbish put out by the citizens who were taxed for the city's expenses: for their part they were forbidden from putting out animal manure or garden weeds with their rubbish. In 1578, a tax was levied on the citizens whose properties were adjacent to the Town Ditch, for it to be kept clean and properly maintained. The work of today's trading standards officers was anticipated with the appointment of ale-tasters and sealers of leather. Other measures for the safety of the city included a survey in 1595, undertaken by the 48 Assistants (the junior members of the city council), split into three groups, to determine levels of occupancy and to reduce overcrowding, and a ban on the use of thatch to reduce the hazard of fire.

At the same time, the council was acquiring property throughout the city, including the Green Croft, which served a variety of purposes: public open space, burial ground for plague victims and place of execution. Not surprisingly, in view of the increase in its wealth and the complexity of its dealings, the council resolved in December 1565 to build new and larger assembly rooms, although work on them was not begun until 1579, and the building was completed only in 1584. It stood in the Market Place, roughly where the War Memorial now stands, and thus directly facing the bishop's guildhall.

With its first floor overhang, to provide space on the ground floor for a covered market, it would have symbolised the council's sense of its own power and a challenge to episcopal authority. That authority could be forcibly expressed, however: Bishop Jewel, an energetic reformer appointed in 1560, had stated in 1565 that 'the Maiour of Sarum was his maiour and the people of Sarum his subjectes'. Then, after about a decade of discussions on a new city charter, and good relations established with the new bishop, John Coldwell, the latter aroused the council's ire in 1593 by speaking of the mayor as 'absolutely his maior'. Following the exchange of writs of ***quo warranto*** the mayor elected in 1594 refused to take his oath of office, and ultimately the dispute remained unresolved.

Meanwhile the council had been careful to cultivate contacts at court, creating a special office of chief steward, whose holders included such highly placed and influential courtiers as Sir Francis Walsingham, Sir Christopher Hatton, Sir Thomas Heneage and Sir John Puckeridge. Both Queen Elizabeth, in 1584, and, on several occasions, James I, were the city's guests. Although at the time the property of Sir Thomas Sadler, the present home of the Salisbury and South Wiltshire Museum is known as the King's House because James I stayed there on his visits to Salisbury. Ultimately, it seems, it was this greater reliance on diplomacy, and arguments based not on conflicting rights but on the dilution of effective leadership resulting from the division of powers between the bishop and the council, which led to the grant of the new charter in 1612.

Salisbury's circumstances had, however, changed out of all recognition since the heady days of John Hall, and by the 17th century it was in no position to capitalise on its new-found freedoms: indeed in the coming century it would need every available advantage to cope with forthcoming challenges.

CHAPTER 5

'THE WORLD TURNED UPSIDE DOWN' 1612–1660

AT THE beginning of the 17th century it must have seemed to many in Salisbury that the future held cause for optimism; that it was, like that of the 20th century, the dawn of a new era. Around the turn of the century there had been years of quiet co-operation with a bishop, Henry Cotton, who was somewhat more amenable than some of his predecessors. Negotiations about a new charter continued, based on the reasonable grounds that the division of powers between bishop and council was hobbling the city's ability to tackle increasing social problems and to regulate its trades effectively. The aim was, as in other cities, for the council to manage its own affairs and to administer its own justice. The costs associated with the final campaign, from 1609 onwards, were met by individual contributions from several hundred of the leading citizens, from 1s up to £5, and a key figure in the drafting of the charter was Giles Tooker, barrister and MP for Salisbury, who became the city's first recorder under its new charter. Also influential was Robert Cecil, first Earl of Salisbury and, at the time of the campaign, Lord High Treasurer.

Thus, in 1612 the city received a charter of incorporation conferring powers to the mayor and council from the king's authority, not the bishop's. While the mayoral oath could still be sworn in the presence of the bishop or his representative, it did not have to be, and although the bishop still had a gaol, stocks and a pillory, his writ ran only as far as the Close. At last, the divisions of power between the episcopal and civil authorities – or the paradoxes inherent in the council's actual power and the bishop's formal authority – were at an end. The question remains how it came to pass that Salisbury failed to develop in the way of other great cities like those of the Midlands and the North, including that other notable mediaeval new town, Kingston-upon-Hull. For the answer we have to consider, first of all, what the council did with its new-found freedom.

The City's New Constitution

As constituted in 1612, the governing body of the city comprised the mayor, elected annually, the recorder, and 24 aldermen with life tenure. Ten of these, with the mayor and recorder, were to be the Justices of the Peace: their powers included the holding of quarter sessions and punishment by death. The corporation also had the power to enact bye-laws. As with justice, the corporation had a powerful grip on the city's economy by virtue of its privilege of appointing the freemen of the city, who had exclusive rights to pursue trades and occupations, and its control over the constitutions of the trade companies. There was to be, as there had been hitherto, a second group, of 48 assistants, who had to reside in the city. The corporation gained the right to acquire land up to the value of £50 annually, and also to administer a number of charities. Apart from the recorder, the city's appointed officers included a clerk to serve both the council and the bench, four 'high constables' to collect the city's rates, two chamberlains to run the city's finances, 13 sub-constables to keep order in the city, three serjeants-at-mace and two beadles.

For the city fathers an early priority was to reorganise the craft guilds into trade companies, which took place in 1612 and 1613. The reconstituted companies included the smiths, comprising armourers, bell-founders, brasiers, cardmakers, cutlers, ironmongers, pewterers, pin-makers, sadlers, watchmakers and wire-drawers; the shoemakers, comprising in addition curriers and last-makers; the grocers, comprising also apothecaries, embroiderers, goldsmiths, linen-drapers, mercers, milliners, upholsterers and vintners; the glovers, including also the collar-makers, parchment-makers and search-makers; then the bakers, cloth-workers, barber-surgeons, silkweavers, and butchers. The last company to be refounded was that of the joiners, which included bellows-makers, bookbinders, carpenters, coopers, instrument makers, masons, mill-wrights, painters, ropemakers, sawyers and turners, wheelwrights and worsted makers. As in earlier times, the range of activities was enormous. The aim of reconstituting the guilds was, however, one of self-preservation. With the economic decline of the last decades of the 16th century, there had been an influx of 'strangers', who had traded without sanction in the city, and this undermining of the city's economy had been one of the causes adduced in support of the petitions to the king for a new charter.

Trade Company Halls: (above) The Joiners' Hall, from Hall's ***Picturesque Memorials***, 1834: unchanged to this day, it is in the care of the National Trust; (below) the Pheasant Inn, incorporating the Shoemakers' Hall, looking much as it does today, in the 1930s.

Thus, among the regulations for the smiths there is one prohibiting the retention of journeymen from outside the city, whether foreign or strangers, without the consent of the wardens of the company, on payment of a daily fine of 12d. This had a parallel in the corporation's order of September 1612 forbidding anyone from practising any trade without being a member of one of the companies, with the sanction of a fine of 40s. Henceforth only those apprenticed in Salisbury were allowed to trade there, and those traders who had gained a foothold in the city without being members of a company were taxed on their property at twice the standard rate. Between the various companies, trading privileges were jealously guarded. Thus, when the bakers and the cooks became two companies in 1620, the former were forbidden from making other than plain bread, except for funerals, and Good Friday and Christmas; nor could they sell bread in the market. As in earlier ages the relationship between the council and the trade companies was both close and symbiotic. The activities of the trade companies provided a significant proportion of the corporation's income, and they were charged with the task of firefighting in the city; at the same time their privileged trading position was supported by the full weight of the corporation's authority. In consequence the city traders were shielded from competition, and so had little incentive to respond to market forces or to develop. In the long run the net result was that Salisbury's pre-eminence in the textile industry was gradually surrendered altogether, and the city's role in manufacturing generally came to assume less importance with the passage of time, yielding place to the travel and service industries. Having failed to seize the initiative when the demand developed for undyed broadcloth, the city's textile workers, having belatedly switched production thereto, persisted in its manufacture when fashion had again changed, by the mid-17th century, in favour of medleys and Spanish cloths.

The Plague

In the early 17th century there were other constraints upon economic growth. These included a run of poor harvests resulting in a 40 per cent increase in the price of wheat between 1626 and 1630, but perhaps most notably there was the plague. Salisbury was visited by the plague in 1563, 1579, and 1604 when it is estimated one in six of the population died. The mechanisms of disease – and particularly the role of sanitation – were poorly understood, and thus, when London succumbed in 1625, Salisbury's only defence was quarantine. It lasted for about two years, but when the first cases occurred in March 1627, anyone who could leave the city did, including most of the corporation. People left the city 'as if it were … an house on fire … until all of any ability were gone, and this in four days'. The clergy barricaded themselves into the Close, and had their food passed over the wall. Within days, there remained only those who could not afford to leave – about 3,000 people – and, of the city's administration, only the mayor, John Ivie, his household and two petty constables. With the plague came looting, starvation, drunkenness and anarchy.

Over 30 years later, when his management of the city's affairs at the time was called into question, Ivie published his ***Declaration***, a rare example of an account of disaster management. In it he explains how, until a rating levy could be raised, and with £80 in cash and a further £300 in credit, he personally underwrote the supply of rations of wheat and barley from a miller in Laverstock, engaged a baker and commissioned the brewers 'to make half-crown beer'. At its peak, his relief operation was producing bread from 27 quarters of wheat, three loads of butter and cheese and 16 hogsheads of beer every week; Ivie continued by providing storehouses, one in each of the three city parishes, for distributing food to the poor, and a pest-house.

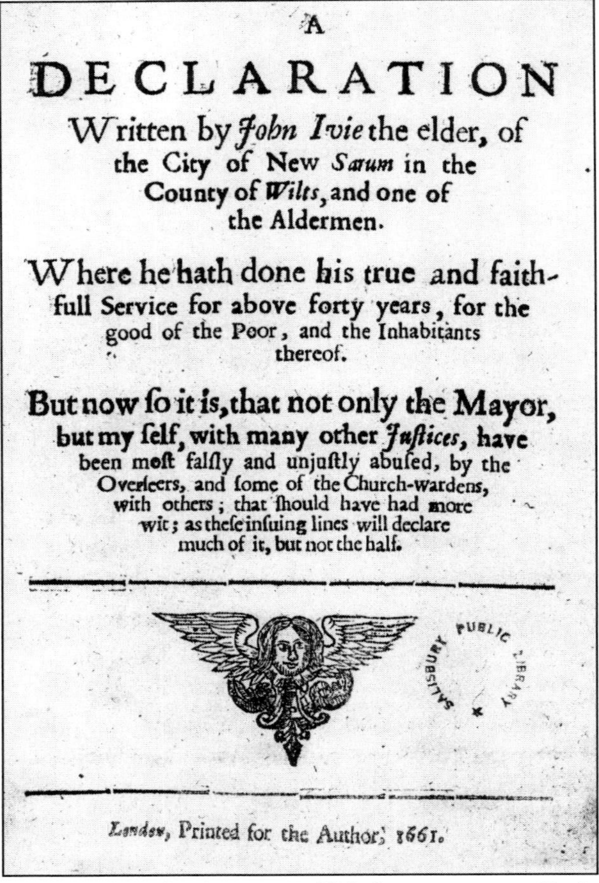

A

DECLARATION

Written by *John Ivie* the elder, of the City of New *Sarum* in the County of *Wilts*, and one of the Aldermen.

Where he hath done his true and faithfull Service for above forty years, for the good of the Poor, and the Inhabitants thereof.

But now so it is, that not only the Mayor, but my self, with many other *Justices*, have been most falsly and unjustly abused, by the Overseers, and some of the Church-wardens, with others; that should have had more wit; as these insuing lines will declare much of it, but not the half.

London, Printed for the Author; 1661.

(Above) Ivie's ***Declaration***. It was published as a quarto pamphlet in 1661 to rebut criticisms of his tenure of the mayoralty during the plague and at other times. In his preface, he exhorts the reader to 'read, without respect to the matter or Author, not poring upon one point, until you understand the whole: and then you shall be able to judge, in the fear of God, the whole intent of the matter and Writer….'; (below) Memorial inscription to John Ivie in the Guildhall, unveiled 1932.

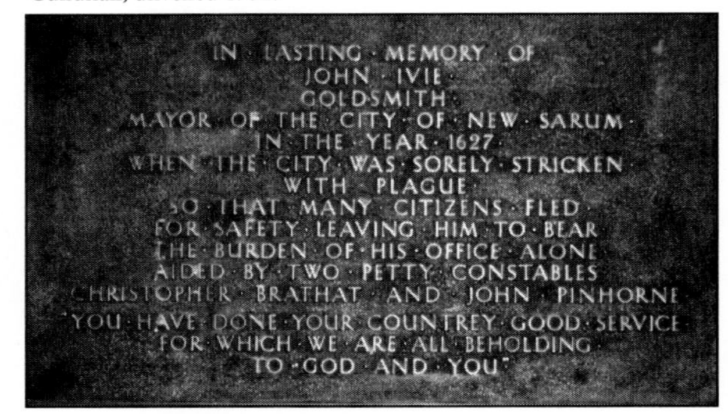

Meanwhile, he had to contend with continued public order offences: Richard Coulter who, with his accomplices, threatened a looting spree if they did not receive greater food rations; Robert Belman who had thrown his neighbour, the wife of a corpse-bearer, out of her home for fear of contracting the plague from her; and Thomas Ravener, an alehouse keeper who mocked his efforts. All these offenders were gaoled. Perhaps most serious was the strike for increased wages by his bearers, which culminated in a siege, followed by the strikers' surrender under gunfire. At times such as this, the only escape from despair in the face of death was drink: Ivie came face to face with a bizarre instance of the consequences when he was called to witness his bearers dancing around the graveyard singing 'Hie for more shoulder-work!'. Ivie's only recourse was to close the alehouses: '… I had suppressed near 100 sellers of drink. By this course I did gain the ill will of thousands …' Only one alehouse keeper, John Chappel, refused to submit: his household and their guests were dead within a week. Ivie commented that 'It pleased God to give me power to suppress all saving that one house; then the God of power did suppress that house in his own judgment'. Divine retribution was similarly visited on some of the tailors who refused to obey Ivie's order not to hold 'their accustomed feast'. Ivie's mettle was to be tested further, when he found that a deranged old woman, the widow Biby, had burnt down the pesthouse. He arrived on the scene to find the 87 inmates 'sitting in the field upon the bare earth, in a miserable condition, many of them almost naked and one quite naked'. He saw to it that the inmates were clothed, and returned them to their homes while the pesthouse was rebuilt. Once back in the new pesthouse, 'but few of them died', recalled Ivie, 'So once more the Lord was pleased to settle that chore.' Eventually the plague subsided: the total death-toll for the city is not known, but for two of the three city parishes it amounted to 369.

The figure represents a dramatic contrast with the 1604 outbreak, when the corresponding figure was 859 and the total 1,007. Clearly, without Ivie's combination of moral courage and organising acumen, the total would have been much greater: the city's debt to him is acknowledged in the name of one of its streets, and a commemorative plaque unveiled in the Guildhall in 1932.

Poor Relief

Ivie's genius and achievement in the relief of urban distress was not confined to emergency measures. The Old Poor Law had, firstly, allowed for the provision of outdoor relief for those incapable of work, of work for those who could, and apprenticeships for the children of the poor, all to be financed by local rates. Begging was forbidden. Secondly, the itinerant poor were to be returned to their place of residence or birth. Lesser provisions in the 1598 legislation tackled the problems of former soldiers and sailors, and the regulation of almshouses. Alongside these mechanisms enshrined in law, many corporations established workhouses, and a law of 1610 ordered the building of houses of correction in every county. It was the kind of problems which these Acts were passed to address that Salisbury had been ill-

Crane Street Workhouse: the courtyard, as portrayed in Hall's ***Picturesque Memorials***, 1834. The city had a workhouse near to St Thomas's church, but the economic hardships of the 1620s and 1630s prompted an expansion of the facilities. It was to remain as the city's workhouse, even after the Poor Law Amendment Act, when the three city parishes were constituted a 'union'. After its closure as a workhouse in 1877, the building was converted and reopened as the diocesan offices (Church House) in 1881.

placed to tackle before the royal charter was granted in 1612, and, both before and after the plague of 1627, which John Ivie and his associates sought to resolve in a variety of ingenious and imaginative ways.

In 1623 a new workhouse was built in St Thomas's Churchyard: as elsewhere it was both workhouse and house of correction, but it also gave substance to the educational intent of the Poor Law by providing training for the children of the destitute. Records of a survey of Salisbury's poor in March 1625 show that 100 children were assigned to masters in the textile and related trades at a bounty of 6d per week each. This arrangement was renewed by a council order in 1626 listing the appropriate occupations, which included sewing, knitting, bone lace-making, pin-making, button-making and spinning. Philip Veryn, a sackcloth and rope-maker, was one such master, and was in 1625 appointed keeper of the workhouse with the brief of training child inmates in dressing and spinning hemp. Again, in 1623, the council borrowed an idea recently attempted in Dorchester, of setting up a municipal brewery, partly to provide employment for the poor, and partly to generate income to defray the costs of poor relief. However, it was opposed by entrenched interests, being patronised by only 18 of the 100 innkeepers in the city. Of its initial costs of £1,500, only £500 had been repaid four years later, and when the undertaking was wound up in 1646, £450 was still outstanding.

Finally, the experiment prompted by the plague, of providing relief in kind through a storehouse, was continued. It was established in Brown Street in December 1628, and it provided essential foodstuffs and fuel in exchange for tokens, and, as with the brewhouse, it was paralleled by an initiative in Dorchester. There were contacts between the corporations and Puritans in many south-western towns, and, indeed, at one time the offices of recorder in Southampton and Salisbury were held simultaneously by Henry Sherfield. When properly run, the storehouse was a success, but like the brewhouse it was brought down by a combination of vested interests, including the overseers of the poor, and incompetent administration. In the ***Declaration***, Ivie notes that while it was in his charge for three and a half years from 1637, 'there was not one beggar seen, either in the Close or the city. At this time the storehouse was let down by the great trouble that was raised by some innkeepers, and alehouses, bakers and hucksters and brewers, and all that loose unruly rabble.' The workhouse expanded, moving into new premises in Crane Street in 1637, where it remained to provide a grim safety-net from the streets until many years after the opening in 1836 of the Alderbury Union workhouse just to the south of the city. In due course its role in training the young was abandoned, dependent as it was on the goodwill and sense of altruism on the part of local employers.

Puritan Conscience and Public Duty

The early 17th century carried over from the previous age the concerns of the Reformation, and, in the process of accommodation between the ferment of ideas and the political settlement, there was inevitably some unfinished business. One of the odder manifestations is to be discovered in the story of the aforementioned Henry Sherfield and the stained glass of St Edmund's Church. Most of Salisbury's stained glass had been removed on the orders of Bishop Jewel in 1567, but somehow a large window in the south aisle, portraying the Creation, had escaped this edict. This had troubled Sherfield for two decades, and he raised the matter at an open meeting of the parish in January 1629. He was granted permission to replace the window, at his own expense, but two of his fellow parishioners succeeded in having the decision referred for approval to the bishop, John Davenant, who refused to sanction the replacement. The matter rankled with Sherfield until he was able, in October 1630, to secrete himself in the church with a pikestaff and set about smashing the window, until he lost his footing, fell, and injured himself so seriously that he had to spend a month indoors. A furore ensued, and on account of his station in life Sherfield was summoned to the Court of Star Chamber in February 1633, where 22 Privy Councillors adjudicated. Sherfield's defence was that, among other things, the Creator had been represented in seven different forms, as of 'little old men in blue and red coats', and that the

The Creation Panel – Swiss glass, early 17th century. Depicting the creation, it was probably acquired after Sherfield's attempt to destroy a window in St Edmund's Church. It was about 12in by 8in, and never mounted in a window, but kept in a wooden frame in the vestry. Lost from historical record for 50 years, it has recently come to light at St Thomas's Church.

Gott erschůff in 6 tagen himel vnd erd
oüch alle die die mögen genämpt werden
gebot dasz man alle wüchen sol 6 tag arb
den 7 firen Růwen vnd sin wort alsó breiten
der gott lept vnd gebüts nach hüt bin dag
das kein manch mit warheit wider sprache
welchem diszem gott alein woll vertrou
der gewüchlich auff den rächen felsen bo
EXODVS AM · XX · CAP
Hans Lässer zů Spreitenbacht
Barbel bruner in Sin Egemahel
1617

Longford Castle was fortified with heavy ordnance by the royalist forces under the king's command, in anticipation of an encounter with Waller's parliamentarian army in the Salisbury area in the late autumn of 1644. This engraving of 1830 shows it in more peaceful surroundings.

sequence of the Creation was misrepresented. Despite his concern and his defence that 'others might offend in idolatry', and that he had broken only those pieces that falsified the Creation story, he was held to have disobeyed the Church, and encroached upon episcopal and thus royal authority. The fine of £500 added to Sherfield's already considerable debts, and he died a broken man less than a year later. As for the window, we have no way of knowing what it looked like or how badly it was damaged, for in June 1653, after the service one Sunday, the tower, which was above the crossing, collapsed and brought down the nave, including the contentious window. What we have today is only the chancel of the old church, with a new tower, built in matching Gothic style during the Commonwealth. At a later date a small panel of Swiss painted glass, representing the creation, was acquired.

Civil War

Meanwhile, the clouds of war had gathered upon the horizon, and in 1642 the Great Rebellion, in Clarendon's phrase, was under way. The west of England, unlike East Anglia, was not uniform in its sympathies. Salisbury was itself divided in its

Lt-General Sir Edmund Ludlow, from his memoirs, published in Vevey, Switzerland, in 1698.

Poultry Cross, ultra-wide angle view. On learning of the presence of the royalist forces, Ludlow headed a troop which rode up the High Street and into Silver Street from the left of this view, and through the gap behind the Poultry Cross to the right, into the Market Place to the attack.

loyalties, the Close, and the city's recorder and one of its MPs, Robert Hyde, being royalist, and the city, and its mayor, Francis Dove, parliamentarian. But perhaps because it had never been properly fortified, its defences being confined to the ramparts, the city was of no great strategic importance, and it was never the object of such bitter conflict as, say, Wardour Castle. That is not to say, however, that Salisbury escaped the rigours of war. From the outset, the mayor worked for the parliamentary cause by raising a troop of militia for the Earl of Pembroke, his efforts aided by a consignment of weapons from Lord Pembroke in addition to those requisitioned from within the city. However, after the battle of Edgehill, Prince Maurice occupied Salisbury, and the mayor was gaoled. Salisbury remained in a kind of no man's land, at risk from whichever side was not in possession of the city. By turns, parliamentary and royalist forces visited the city, sometimes simply passing through, sometimes raiding the city for valuables or to extort fines and protection money.

In fact Salisbury's only real taste of conflict came shortly after Colonel Coke's garrison, ensconced in the Close, was captured in December 1644 by a detachment of Sir Edmund Ludlow's parliamentary forces; in due course the belfry was garrisoned and adopted as

The belfry with a spire, as it would have looked at the time when it became Ludlow's command-post in January 1645.

Ludlow's command-post. In January, Ludlow learned of an impending counter-attack. On reconnaissance in Winchester Street, he found that the royalists under Sir Marmaduke Langdale had entered the city from the north: doubling back, he found they had already reached the Market Place, and escaped via New Canal to rejoin his garrison in the Close. Ludlow split his 30-strong force into two, and sent an advance party to attack the royalist forces. He followed with the remainder, filing through the gap into the Market Place between the Poultry Cross and the angle between Oatmeal and Ox Rows, with much sounding of cornets to suggest the marshalling of larger forces. The ruse succeeded, and the royalists broke into two groups, one of which fled up Winchester Street, and the other, numbering about 200, retreated into Endless Street: despite its name, a cul-de-sac. Ludlow and his men were forced back to the Close, and finding from intelligence that he was outnumbered by around 30 to one, he escaped to Harnham in search of reinforcements. He returned to find Langdale's force occupying the Close, with one detachment beating his troop back in the direction of Harnham and safety and the other enlisting the services of a passing charcoal-carrier to burn down the belfry doors and smoke out Lt-Col. Read's contingent. In the process the carrier lost his life. The escaping force under Ludlow scattered across the fields: when challenged, Ludlow shot his way out of capture and travelled alone to Southampton.

Once the royalists were firmly in command of the city, their troops went on the rampage for three days, earning the censure of parliamentarians and royalists alike. The record of their depredations makes for sorry reading: John Jeffreys was relieved of property worth £17 5s, Thomas Lawes' losses included £20-worth of wine; William Autram and William Phillips were raided several times; one widow Ranlington, in need of constant nursing, was relieved of the wherewithal for her care, and Thomas Kynton's house was left practically bare.

Colonel John Penruddock.

The Commonwealth and After

Within a few weeks the city was free of the royalists, and within a few months it had welcomed Cromwell himself, who visited Salisbury in May and October. The Commonwealth appears to have ushered in an era not unlike China's Cultural Revolution, with Quakers and alleged witches treated with indifferent harshness. Of the former, Katherine Evans was whipped for urging her hearers to 'flee the wrath that is to come', and dismissed from the city, only to return and be imprisoned for a repeat offence. Of the latter, Anne Bodenham of Fisherton was executed for having at her beck five spirits appearing as ragged boys, and for turning herself into a cat. With the abolition of the episcopacy, the estates of the dean and chapter became state property to be disposed of by sale: the corporation paid £880 for four canonries to provide accommodation for puritan ministers for the cathedral and the three city parish churches. The Bishop's Palace, similarly acquired, was divided up, one tenement becoming an inn. The cathedral precincts were turned over to secular purposes: a rubbish dump and slaughter-yard, and the cloisters and library housed Dutch prisoners of war in 1653. All the while, however, the cathedral fabric was maintained at the expense of local benefactors.

It is not surprising that by 1655 the dour regime of the Protectorate should have inspired a rebellion; the tragedy was that only five years after its collapse, the monarchy was restored. The aim of its instigators, colonels John Penruddock of Compton Park and Hugh Grove of Chisenbury Priors, can be summarised as raising enough armed support to capture the towns of the west. Penruddock hoped and believed (or at least asserted) that similar insurrections were taking place throughout the country and that an invasion force of 10,000 men headed by the Duke of York was on its way from France. In fact, there was little support for the idea, the king in exile doubting the conspirators' chances, and promises of help along the way failing to materialise. Once embarked upon, there was no turning back. Starting at Clarendon on 11 March, the rebels marched on Salisbury with about 200 troops, and succeeded in capturing the Assize judges and the High Sheriff of Wiltshire, and opening the gaol to recruit some of the inmates to the cause. After releasing the judges, the rebels rode west, abandoning their hostage the High Sheriff at Yeovil on 13 March. They reached South Molton, Devon on the 14th, by this time reduced to about 100, and there they were cornered by Captain Unton Crook and his cavalry who had come from Exeter.

After some hours' fighting, the rebel force surrendered on Crook's assurance that they would not be harmed, and were subsequently committed to Exeter Gaol. At the resumed Assizes in Salisbury, the judges handed down justice to their erstwhile captors, who came from such diverse trades as vintner, ostler, tailor, spurrier and soapboiler: by no means were the rebels exclusively landed gentry. Twenty-three were on trial for treason, another seven faced charges of highway robbery or horse-stealing: seven were executed and others were banished into slavery on the plantations. Penruddock was tried in Exeter, and found guilty after 15 minutes of deliberation. Like his supporters in Salisbury he was executed on 3 May 1655. Penruddock's rise and fall are commemorated in a contemporary broadside ballad:

You gallant English men that be
Of valeur and courageous mind,
I'de wish you have a speciall care
To what concets you are inclin'd.
A sad and mournful precedent
Ile here lay to your publick view,
Whereby all men may understand
What here is printed to be true.
Grove and Penruddock did rebell,
But now they bid the world farewel.

The lives and deaths of two brave men
Shall in plain terms be now exprest,
Who were beheaded at Exeter,
A famous Citie in the West.
Colonel Penruddock was the one,
A Souldier of couragious worth,
And Captain Grove a Gentleman
Whose name fame's trumpet sounded forth.
Grove and Penruddock did rebell,
But now they bid the world farewel.

Within a few years the monarchy was restored, and Salisbury had its second new beginning in a century. There were to be faint echoes both of rebellion and of civil war, with Monmouth's rebellion in June 1685 finding little sympathy and no support. Three and a half years later the city was equally warm in its welcomes by turns to James II, who chose Salisbury to be his headquarters, and Prince William of Orange, when the king had fled.

Chapter 6

'A stately and rich Plainenesse' – Restoration and Georgian Salisbury

THE Restoration ushered in a new era of gentility in the life and fortunes of the city: throughout the remainder of the 17th century and the whole of the 18th Salisbury became to a significant degree the city we have today. The vicissitudes of the previous half-century had pushed Salisbury down to being the 15th largest of England's cities, but its position in the transport network between London and the West Country and the continuing presence of a coterie of cultured and influential individuals were key factors in what John Chandler has identified as the process by which Salisbury reinvented itself, to become 'gentrified'.

Bishop Ward and his Circle

Prominent in this process were the Anglican clergy, who soon reoccupied the Close after 1662, and were joined in 1667 by the new bishop, Seth Ward. Prior to his appointment, Ward had been Savilian Professor of Astronomy at Oxford, had published both scientific and religious treatises, including ***De Astronomia Geometrica*** (1656), and had, through his membership of the Philosophical Society of Oxford, become a founding father of the Royal Society. When his academic career was thwarted by Cromwell, Ward pursued his religious vocation, rising within a few years to the bishopric of Exeter. His tenure at Salisbury was distinguished not only by his efforts within the Close and the diocese, but also by his circle of friends. Soon after his appointment he invited Christopher Wren, a friend since he had been Ward's student at Oxford, to appraise the condition of the cathedral's fabric. Wren found little to criticise and much to admire in the cathedral, commenting:

> The Pillars and the Spaces between them are well suited to the highth of the Arches, the Mouldings are decently mixed with large planes without an affectation of filling every corner with ornaments, which (unlesse they are admirably good) glut the eye, as much as in Musick, too much Division cloyes the eare, the Windowes are not made too great, nor yet the light obstructed with many mullions and transomes of Tracery-worke which was the ill fashion of the next [i.e. following] age. Our Artist knew better that nothing could add beauty to light, he trusted in a stately and rich Plainenesse.

Christopher Wren, Ward's friend and adviser regarding the structure of the cathedral.

Seth Ward, bishop of Salisbury, 1667–1689.

In fact Wren's suggestions were confined to refurnishing the choir and repairing the spire, with a watching brief being maintained on the latter through the suspension of a plumbline. In addition to these works, Ward paved the cloisters and the choir with black and white marble, and repaired his palace at a personal cost of more than £2,000. Within the diocese he travelled widely, to acquaint himself with, and where necessary improve, the circumstances of his parish clergy. His concern is borne out by the College of Matrons dating from 1682, and so named deliberately to emphasise the gentility of its beneficiaries. The college was a group of almshouses for 12 clergy widows from the sees of Exeter and Salisbury, founded by Ward, it is said, on learning that a lady who had rejected his suit in favour of another clergyman had been reduced in her widowhood to a state of penury. Ward was also mindful of the prosperity of the city – a concern which went far in conciliating the corporation's sense of ***amour propre*** in its relations with the dean and chapter. In 1672 he helped substantially to underwrite the project to render the River Avon navigable from Christchurch to Salisbury, the main problems being in the reaches around Britford. The many difficulties were finally resolved by 1684, and the scheme came to fruition when two 25-ton wherries docked by Ayleswade Bridge.

Among Ward's circle of friends who were associated with him at Salisbury, Isaac Barrow, who had resigned the Lucasian Professorship in mathematics at Cambridge in favour of Isaac Newton (another of Ward's protégés) and was later to become Master of Trinity College, Cambridge, was for a time Ward's chaplain, and a canon and prebendary in the cathedral. His guests included Robert Boyle and Samuel Pepys, who visited the city in 1668, and his neighbours in the Close included Izaak Walton and Dr Daubeney Turberville. Walton was the son of the author of ***The Compleat Angler***, while Turberville was an eye surgeon who moved to Salisbury from London. Ward's biographer, Walter Pope, asserted that the innkeepers who put his patients up were as much the beneficiaries of his presence as the afflicted who visited Salisbury, 'being dispersd thro' all the quarters of the city, insomuch, that once could scarce peep out of doors, but he had a prospect of some led by boys ... others with bandages over one, or both eyes, and yet a greater number wearing green Silk upon their Faces, which if a Stranger should see ... I should not wonder if he believd and reported the Air of Salisbury to be as pernicious to the Eyes as that of Orleans is to the Nerves, where almost one third of the Inhabitants are Lame.'

New Building in the Close and the City

The gentrification of the Close as a social phenomenon was accompanied by increasing architectural elegance. The process of relinquishing canonries to secular occupancy has already been remarked upon; it became far more widespread after the Reformation and during the Civil War, when the Anglican clergy were dispossessed. The land on which Mompesson House stood was an early instance of properties in the Close passing into lay hands, for it was leased to Thomas Sharpe in 1565. The Mompesson association dates from 1635, when it was rented at an annual charge of 8s 4d by the grandfather of the builder of the present house, Charles Mompesson. His father had been one of the supporters of Penruddock's rebellion, but had managed to escape; at the Restoration he embarked on a career in Parliament, and was, with Ward, one of the supporters of the Avon

College of Matrons: Seth Ward's almshouses for clergy widows from the sees of Salisbury and Exeter.

Navigation scheme. Like his father, Charles represented Old Sarum and Wilton in Parliament.

The present house was built in 1701, and is a classical example of a William and Mary town house. It was, however, by no means the earliest example of new building in the Close in the later 17th century, which began with the building of No.7 before 1660, and continued with No.14 shortly after 1662. However,

College of Matrons: the inscription explaining the foundation of the college.

Mompesson House, home of the Mompesson family from when it was built until the late 1730s.

Arundells, so named after a tenant in the 1740s, the Hon. James Everard Arundell, a son of the 6th Lord Arundell of Wardour. The house was restored as a labour of love by Robert and Kate Hawkings in 1964 and since 1985 has been the home of Sir Edward Heath, who, as the Hawkingses relate, acquired the freehold 'using little-known legislation … from a very unhappy Dean and Chapter. They could ill-afford to lose in this way one of the most valuable and important houses in the close.'

Mathematical tiles, used as a facing material to imitate brick, seen here on a property in Catherine Street, and with slate-hanging – once a facing material characteristic of Salisbury – now, like mathematical tiles, rarely to be seen.

these, like their antecedents from earlier in the century, were relatively domestic in scale, and Mompesson House was in the vanguard of a series of aristocratic houses, either completely new or remodellings of pre-existing properties.

The process of transformation of the Close continued throughout the 18th century. It began with the remodelling of what is now Malmesbury House in 1705, of Braybrooke after 1706, of Arundells and Leadenhall around 1720, and the building from scratch of Myles Place between 1718 and 1722, and of its neighbour the Walton Canonry around 1720.

The architectural and social reinvention of the Close in the century after the Restoration had its parallel across the city. The most distinguished example is Bourne Hill, now the headquarters offices of the District Council, but previously the home of the Wyndham family, from 1657. Its present handsome façade dates from the mid-18th century, and extensive additions were made in 1790. Second only to Bourne Hill is The Hall in New Street, built on the site of the Assembly House for William Hussey, clothier, alderman, MP for

Bourne Hill, as 'The College' the home of the Wyndham family from 1660 until it was sold in 1871, subsequently to become a school under the direction of Dr G.H. Bourne (whence its present name), from whom it passed to the City (now District) Council in 1927, to become its administrative centre.

Salisbury from 1774 to 1813 and benefactor of the almshouses which bear his name. There are many other 18th-century town houses in Salisbury, including some in Cheese Market and in Castle and Endless Streets, and more in St Ann Street. Throughout the city older houses were often given a modern frontage with the addition of a facing of brickwork or 'mathematical' tiles. These were designed to be used as a cladding on vertical surfaces and were profiled so that they presented a plane surface, which could be pointed with mortar to give the appearance of brick, while being free of the tax levied on brickwork from 1784 to 1850. Examples can be found in Crane Street, High Street, Catherine Street and Queen Street.

Visitors' Impressions

As well as being somewhere to live, Salisbury was somewhere to visit, as it had been since mediaeval times, but now for social and sightseeing reasons. Even before the turnpike roads were built Salisbury was at the centre of a substantial network of roads, with routes converging on the city from London, Southampton, Blandford Forum, Shaftesbury, Bath, and Marlborough. Salisbury's earliest visitors included royalty: Charles II and his retinue stayed in Salisbury from July until September 1665 to avoid the plague, and in 1669 Prince Cosimo de Medici of Tuscany visited the city while staying with the Earl of Pembroke at Wilton. Others included the diarists John Evelyn, Celia Fiennes and Samuel Pepys. Evelyn, Fiennes and the narrator of Cosimo's visit all mention the watercourses: Evelyn remarked that the water flowed quite swiftly along the channels, but that the streets were neglected and dirty for want of a modest outlay in maintenance, sentiments echoed by Miss Fiennes.

But while Cosimo and Wren were struck by the beauty of the cathedral and the inexplicable grandeur of Stonehenge, Miss Fiennes remarks on the abundance of provisions and the regular supply in the market of 'fruite, fowle, butter and cheese and a fish Market'. Writing some 20 years later, Daniel Defoe was as scathing as Evelyn about the state of the watercourses, but remarked particularly on the 'great variety of manufactures', including the specialist manufacture of textiles: fine-quality flannels and 'long cloths for the Turkey [i.e. near eastern] trade, call'd Salisbury whites'.

The Textile Trades in the 17th and 18th Centuries

Still of significance, though no longer the engine of economic development, the textile trade had gained a reprieve by finding a niche market. However, a combination of the unreliability of overseas markets, unfavourable legislation (which prompted a whole series of petitions to Parliament) and French competition killed off the trade in whites and crippled that for flannels. Only by producing other speciality textiles – the mottled marble cloths which were peculiar to Salisbury and Wilton, and the cassimeres, a type of cloth invented only in 1766 – did the Salisbury cloth trade manage to survive, although silk and velvet were important specialities in the 17th and 18th centuries. There was a final resurgence in the textile trade towards the end of the 18th century. Production of flannels revived, stimulated by exports to France, Germany, North America and the East Indies, and other specialities such as fancy cloths, linsey-woolsey, pepper-and-salt, striped cloth, swan's-down, and toilinette were produced, as were serge and blanketing. Royal patronage, bestowed when Thomas Ogden was appointed draper to George III in 1786, sparked off a vogue for Salisbury produce and the arrival of the spinning jenny by 1777 heralded the benefits of mechanisation. Revolution in France and the ensuing collapse of the French export trade initially played to Salisbury's advantage. Demand was so heavy that in 1791 Henry Wansey, one of the foremost producers, was compelled to decline business. By late in the century the textile trades accounted for about a quarter of the city's workers. ***Bailey's Western and Midland Directory*** of 1783 lists 33 businessmen in the textile trades and the ***Universal British Directory*** of 1798 lists 27 clothiers and clothes-shopkeepers, and 48 involved in the mainstream textile trades.

Cutlery and Bone-Lace – Two Salisbury Specialities

Other trades which prospered, doubtless aided by the attraction which Salisbury held for visitors, were cutlery and bone-lace manufacture. Philip Luckombe, author

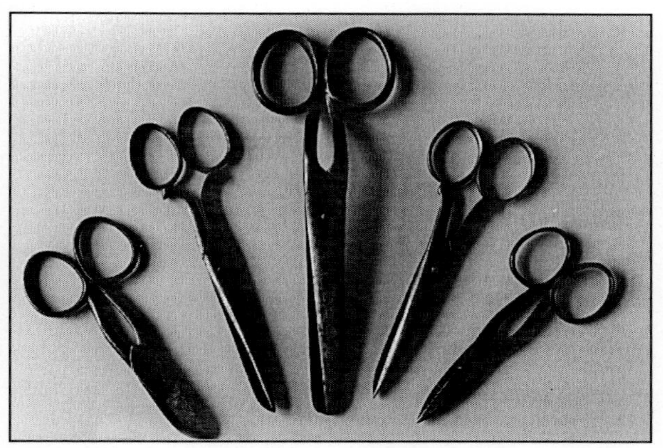

Scissors: the two pairs on the left were made by Beach, the centre pair has no maker's name, the two pairs on the right were made by Macklin.

of ***England's gazetteer*** (1790) cites both of these as Salisbury specialities. Cutlery was never a mass manufacture, even by pre-industrial standards, but it was a luxury trade, patronised by royalty and their close associates. It was said that Nell Gwyn visited Salisbury and paid 100 guineas for a pair of scissors, while a guidebook to Bath contained the couplet 'Let Bristol for commerce and dirt be renowned/At Salisbury let penknives and scissors be ground'. The directory of 1783, and his own trade-card, describe M. Goddard as cutler to the King, Queen and Prince of Wales. Cutlery was also cited as a speciality of the city in the earliest guidebooks, and it is said that passengers on the London and Exeter coach were offered cutlery, with sales of up to £70 per coach. In the ***Salisbury Guide*** of 1814 Easton extolled its virtues thus: 'The manufacture of cutlery in this place is brought to the highest degree of perfection, and supposed infinitely to excel all others, the fine temperature of the steel being attributed to the peculiar quality of the water.' Bone-lace, another luxury product, made throughout Wiltshire and Dorset, was gathered together by merchants who then sold it in Salisbury, but the city itself was a centre of manufacture as well as of trade and retail distribution, throughout the 17th and 18th centuries. The work was done by women and children: 18th-century apprenticeship records mention only three for lacemaking, and apprentices and masters were all female. By 1700 around 1,000, or a seventh of the population, were lace-makers, but the trade was handled by men of substance. One dealer supplied the London market with around £70-worth of lace per week in around 1700, and in 1681 Salisbury had had a laceman, Richard Minifie, as its mayor.

(Above) Downton lace. There is no extant piece of Salisbury lace, but the industry passed to Downton, where it was made in the same way. The piece illustrated is a tribute to the Queen on the occasion of her coronation; (below) Bobbin-lace maker demonstrating her craft, Salisbury and South Wiltshire Museum, August 2002.

The City's Infrastructure

As trade and communications developed, driven to a significant degree by the demands of increasingly prosperous middle and upper classes, so both the city's infrastructure and its social and environmental ambience evolved. We have noted the beginning of these processes above, and they continued throughout the 18th century. As in the previous century, the city was vulnerable to disease: there were no further plague epidemics, but severe outbreaks of smallpox occurred in 1723, 1752 and 1766. Between the latter two outbreaks an appeal was launched for a smallpox hospital, and Viscount Folkestone, afterwards Earl of Radnor, gave a house in Bugmore for the purpose in 1763. The family connection was maintained when in the same year his father-in-law, Lord Feversham, bequeathed £500 for the establishment of a general county hospital, on condi-

Engraving of the front elevation of the Infirmary: a 19th-century bird's-eye view by Frank Highman.

tion it came into being within five years. In fact the new Infirmary admitted its first patients in 1767.

In 1737, in response to a petition from the corporation and the people of Salisbury, an act was passed for the upkeep of the city's thoroughfares. The first of its kind for a provincial city, it was a precursor to today's Public Utilities and Street Works Acts. One outcome was that the watercourses were diverted to brick-lined channels at the side of the carriageway. The new channels were about 2ft deep and 2ft across, and water flowed to a depth of 12-18in. At intervals there were footbridges, and early 19th-century engravings of Minster Street and High Street give a good impression of their appearance. Access for wheeled traffic was greatly facilitated, and the city took a major step in evolving from the English Venice to its present-day look. The first few street lamps had been erected in 1727 to celebrate the coronation of George II, and were the gift of one of the city's MPs. Altogether there were 23, including four in the Market Place; others were set up on bridges, and more were set up in 1769.

Roads and Travel

An important development outside the city was the improvement of the road network by the turnpike trusts, although the earliest trust on a Salisbury route was only founded in 1753, and it was a further 30 years before all of the major roads to Salisbury were turnpiked. Once they were, the effect was dramatic. Arthur Young described the road to Romsey, part of the Sarum and Eling Turnpike, as being like 'an elegant gravel walk'. The frequency of stage-coach services increased, one commentator on the London–Exeter service in 1773 observing that 'whereas about 10 years ago there passed through the city, in the course of a week … six stage-coaches, each carrying six passengers, at present there constantly pass in the same time 24 coaches and 28 stage-chaises, making on the whole 228 passengers'. Improvements in the road and in coach design cut the journey time between London and Exeter via Salisbury from four days in 1658 to 32 hours by the 1780s. Easton's ***Salisbury Guide*** of 1769 lists nearly eighty destinations served by stage-coaches and carriers, ranging from major cities such as Exeter, Plymouth, Oxford and Bristol to villages and towns throughout Wiltshire, Hampshire and Dorset: Donhead and Wardour, Frome, Hindon and 'Shipton-Mallard'. A city such as Bath was accessible by five services which between them travelled out on four days, each returning the following day. A service to the capital was offered by the 'Salisbury Machine – For London, sets out from the Red Lion and Cross-Keys, Monday, Wednesday and Friday, at three o'Clock in the Morning: returns Tuesday, Thursday, and Saturday, in the Afternoon'.

The association between travel and inns appears axiomatic, but in the heyday of the stage-coach, when journeys often involved overnight stays and the larger inns were designed to accommodate coaches and offer stabling, it was a far closer relationship than is often the case today. Just how important travel was to Salisbury's economy, even as early as the 1680s, has been shown by John Chandler, who has compared a War Office survey of 1686, compiled to provide billeting data, with a near-contemporary religious census. His comparison shows that Fisherton Anger, in effect Salisbury's western suburb, could offer one bed for the night for every 1.4 head of population. The figure for Salisbury proper is 1:2.4, two-and-a-half times the capacity of Trowbridge or Marlborough.

The Bankrupt Canal

In the light of the effectiveness of the road transport system, it is perhaps not surprising that the technical difficulties attendant on maintaining the Avon Navigation resulted in the project's abandonment. The natural river flow could not be relied upon to provide sufficient draught for barges as a canal would have done. Latterly the lock system at Britford was adapted for irrigating the water meadows. There was a later attempt to build a canal between Salisbury and Southampton, which might eventually have contributed to an inland waterway system to link Southampton to Bristol. When the idea was first mooted in 1770 following the success of the Duke of Bridgewater's Manchester Canal, it was claimed that £3,000 could be saved annually in transport costs for the city's coal. But while resumed initiatives at the height of the canal boom in the 1790s resulted in the building of the canal (or canalised river) joining Andover and Redbridge, the attempt to graft onto this the two links across to Salisbury and down to Southampton foundered in the face of engineering problems insuperable with the available funds. There was something of a portent in the inaugural public meeting at Southampton on 27 December 1792, when, of the 89 would-be subscribers to the scheme, in contrast to the 70 from Bristol and Southampton, only 4 from Salisbury stepped forward. The capital raised had been £56,000, but the canal had only reached Dean when this figure was exhausted and the project declared bankrupt. A proposal to revive the scheme in 1824 came to nothing: perhaps by then the potential of the railways was evident.

(Left) James Harris, father of the first Earl of Malmesbury, author and patron of Handel. (Below) Title-page to libretto of Handel's *Acis and Galatea*, published locally for performances in Salisbury.

THE MASQUE OF ACIS AND GALATEA.

SALISBURY: Printed by B. COLLINS, on the NEW CANAL, 1762. [Price SIX-PENCE]

The Press, Music and Drama

Another consequence of improved roads, central to the life of the city, was the development of journalism. From the earliest beginnings in 1620, the Civil War prompted an explosive growth in the spread of ideas and information through cheaply-produced pamphlets and newspapers: Ivie's ***Declaration*** belongs to that tradition. But, as a result of the Printing Act of 1662, which limited presses to London and York, and Oxford and Cambridge universities, it was to be many decades before regular resumés of local current affairs were launched. The first such attempts were in Norwich and Exeter, and were followed by the short-lived ***Salisbury Post Man*** of 1715. The ***Salisbury Journal*** was first published in 1729, and suffered two abortive runs before being relaunched in 1738, since when it has appeared weekly. Originally printed on a single folio sheet, it comprised four hand-set pages, and in the early years of the 19th century cost 7d – more than a day's wage for many at the time, of which 4d was Government stamp duty. Salisbury's affairs were broadcast to the world, for the ***Journal*** was read in London coffee-houses. As its reputation and circulation grew it was renamed the ***Salisbury and Winchester Journal*** in 1772, in competition with Jacob and Johnson's ***Hampshire Chronicle***, first published in that

SALISBURY.

ELIZABETH FISHLAKE, Cork Cutter, near the Lamb Inn, Catherine-ſtreet, reſpectfully informs her friends, that ſhe has juſt received a quantity of the beſt Whitby Barrel Cod Salt Fiſh: She has likewiſe Oranges and Lemons, Piſtachio Nuts and Spaniſh Cheſnuts, Whole and Split Peaſe, Brawn, Red and White Herrings of the beſt quality, wholeſale and retail, on the moſt reaſonable terms. A continuation of the favours of her friends, &c. will be gratefully acknowledged, by their moſt humble ſervant,

ELIZABETH FISHLAKE.

Advert for Elizabeth Fishlake, the cork-cutter, a resourceful woman who had a great many other strings to her bow than cutting cork, *Salisbury Journal*, 12 February 1781.

year. In addition, however, the affairs of the world were brought to the people of Salisbury, for the ***Journal*** carried national news from its inception until just after World War One. It was joined by other papers in the 19th century, including ***Simpson's Salisbury Gazette***, from 1816 to 1819, the forerunner of the ***Devizes and Wiltshire Gazette***, and, from 1868 onwards, by the ***Salisbury Times***. Among the ***Journal's*** earliest national stories were the capture of Dick Turpin and the Battle of Culloden. A major source of its income came from advertising, and the front page and much of the inside space was devoted thereto. The issue dated 27 December 1784 contains the following comic verses celebrating its advertising:

> If any gem'man wants a wife
> (A partner, as 'tis termed for life)
> An advertisement does the thing
> And quickly brings the pretty thing.
>
> If you want health, consult our pages,
> You shall be well, and live for ages;
> Our empirics, to get them bread,
> Do everything – but raise the dead!
>
> Lands may be had, if they are wanted;
> Annuities of all sorts are granted;
> Placements, preferments, bought and sold;
> Houses to purchase, new and old.
>
> Ships, shops, of every shape and form,
> Carriages, horses, servants swarm;
> No matter whether good or bad,
> We tell you where they must be had.
>
> Our services you can't express,
> The good we do you hardly guess;
> There's not a want of human kind,
> But we a remedy can find.

The success of the ***Journal's*** publication allowed its proprietor, Benjamin Collins, to venture into general publishing, and indeed Salisbury became a provincial centre for publishing, distinctive in its range and diversity. Among Collins's other publications were libretti for the performances of Handel's works, including ***Acis and Galatea*** and ***Judas Maccabeus***, and the first edition of Goldsmith's ***The Vicar of Wakefield***, while Edward

Silhouette of Benjamin Banks.

Easton's publishing output covered an enormous range, from the ***Salisbury Guide***, which first appeared in 1769 and ran to 31 editions by 1830, to a three-volume Spanish text edition of Cervantes's ***Don Quixote***, to the philosophical and philological writings of James Harris. The market for such an output is one reflection of a cultured society; Harris's patronage of Handel is another. He was a prime mover in the musical life of the city, including the annual musical festivals on St Cecilia's day which featured Handel's works including ***Saul*** and ***Jephtha***, and a series of subscription concerts. In regular contact with Harris for over 20 years until his death in 1759, Handel was also Harris's house guest in 1740, giving an impromptu recital at a private concert staged by Harris. Musical life was sufficiently vigorous to support the livelihoods of Benjamin Banks, a stringed-instrument maker renowned for his violins, from 1747 to 1795, and of Henry Costar, an organ-builder and harpsichord maker listed in the directory of 1783. The theatre, too, flourished in Salisbury: the ***Salisbury Guide*** of 1769 notes 'We have a pretty Theatre at the Vine, and are visited by a Company of Players every year'. In the season of 1751–2 the programme included a Shakespeare cycle, featuring ***Hamlet, King Lear, Othello*** and ***Romeo and Juliet***; the following year, Sheridan's ***The Recruiting Officer*** was performed. Two other theatres were founded in the later 18th century: by 1765 the Sun Inn, next to Fisherton Bridge, had its own theatre. Then in 1777 the New Theatre opened, heralding the arrival of the theatre in a more permanent sense, in that it was a custom-designed building with its own repertory company which also toured Southampton, Winchester and Chichester. Its opening production was Sheridan's ***The Rivals***.

Restoration of the Cathedral

Perhaps the most enduring manifestations of Salisbury's 'gentrification' are in the built environment, within the Close and in the Market Place. Those in the Close were undertaken at the instigation of Bishop Shute Barrington, an energetic reformer who had been appointed in 1782 and who in 1789 called upon James Wyatt, the most celebrated architect of the day, to restore the cathedral: to purge it of the excrescences which clouded the prospect of its original conception. Wyatt's work took three years and upon the reopening, attended by the King at a service which included the 'Hallelujah Chorus', was widely acclaimed. Yet ever since, Wyatt's reputation has been tarnished by the association with work for which he was not the prime mover and with which he had considerable misgivings. His work impinged upon the exterior and interior environments. Externally, the major change was the demolition of the belfry, which had housed a ring of at least 10 and possibly 12 bells, most of which had been sold by 1777. By the time of Wyatt's commission the building was in a state of some disrepair, and it was seen as a blot on the landscape, obscuring the view which the cathedral presented to the world. The other radical alteration was the raising and levelling of the graveyard, entailing the removal of the tombstones and the filling in of the watercourse traversing the Close. Internally, the main changes comprised the rearrangement of the tombs into rows between the nave piers, the removal of the mediaeval glass and the whitewashing of the vaulting, the rebuilding of the choir screen and the demolition of the 15th-century chantry chapels built into the angles between the eastern transepts and the Trinity Chapel.

James Wyatt, commissioned to oversee and direct the restoration of the cathedral.

Shute Barrington, bishop of Salisbury 1782–1791.

To a later age and still by present-day standards the restoration entailed much to be regretted. William Beckford, one of Wyatt's clients, described the newly-restored cathedral as looking like a 'scantily-clad whore', and from the time of Pugin, a leading figure in both the Anglo-Catholic movement and its counterpart in architecture, the Gothic revival, Wyatt's memory has been execrated, mainly with Pugin's epithet 'The Destroyer'.

From Hall's ***Picturesque memorials***, 1834, the Beauchamp and Hungerford chantries, demolished in Wyatt's restoration. Both were neglected, and the Hungerford chantry seems to have been used as a lumber room in its later years.

Wall painting in the Hungerford Chantry, lost when it was demolished.

The ahistorical nature of these judgements is not hard to demonstrate. The saddest losses were of the chantry chapels, the choir screen and the glass. But the construction of the chantries had entailed cutting tomb-recesses in the walls of the Trinity Chapel, and they were regarded on structural as well as artistic grounds as compromising the integrity of the main building; the Hungerford Chantry in particular was in a neglected and weakened condition. Wyatt's screen had to support the new organ, the gift of the King, and on it he incorporated carving from the chantries, as he did that from the original screen into the Morning Chapel. Finally, the mediaeval glass, probably darkened over the centuries, caused the interior of the cathedral to be bathed in a 'dim, religious light': nowadays, like the chantries, it would doubtless have been restored. In the 18th century there was no such concept, and indeed in all his work Wyatt was striving to recapture the unity and grace of Elias de Dereham's original conception.

As for the Close, it had been described by John Byng in 1782 as 'like a cow-common, as dirty and as neglected, and thro' the centre stagnates a boggy ditch'. A contemporary engraving shows the Close being used for that very purpose. Had it not been tidied up at the time, it undoubtedly would have been later. Yet the clearing of the graveyard was so unpopular that it had to be carried out under cover of darkness, and incurred the opprobrium of the city council to the extent that it withdrew its financial support for the restoration. However, it has left the cathedral with the finest setting of any in the country. The one major loss – the view of the cathedral from the south – arose from Barrington's commandeering part of the Close to add to the grounds of his palace; and in that theft from future generations Wyatt played no part whatsoever. The constant need for maintenance and changing tastes in subsequent eras led to a further restoration, equally thoroughgoing, between 1862 and 1879 under the direction of Sir George Gilbert Scott. The restoration included the installation of some 80 new statues on the west front, the repainting of the vaulting of the choir and presbytery, and the replacement of Wyatt's choir screen.

A rare photograph of the nave of the cathedral showing Wyatt's screen.

(Above) Entrance to the Beauchamp Chantry, now preserved in the Morning Chapel in the north-eastern transept. (Below) Carving from the mediaeval choir screen, which Wyatt placed in the Morning Chapel in the north-eastern transept.

Views down the nave. (Above) From Hall's ***Picturesque memorials***, 1834. At the time of the print's publication this was an historic view, recording the view 80 years earlier, and thus before Wyatt's work. The font is now in Yankalilla, South Australia. (Below) the wrought-iron screen installed during Scott's restoration.

Scott had wished to reinstate a stone choir screen like the one Wyatt had removed, but was constrained by the terms of the gift of Dean Lear's widow to commission Francis Skidmore to fashion one of wrought iron. This, in turn, was removed in the last century, affording us the uninterrupted view down the nave to the high altar which we have today.

The view today, without any interruptions.

The End of the Council House and the Building of the Guildhall

The transformation of the Market Place to something like its present appearance resulted ultimately from a fire after a mayoral banquet on 16 November 1780. Despite reports, often repeated subsequently, of a great conflagration, the fire was brought under control within four hours, even with the primitive methods of fire-fighting then available. The building remained intact, and although its upper stories were badly damaged, repairs were quickly put in hand. The ***Salisbury Journal***, 11 December 1780, reported that work was well enough advanced for the building to be ready for the January Assizes, which were duly held there. But the building was perceived to be an even bigger eyesore than before the fire, and in its pristine state it had been held in no great admiration. The ***Salisbury Guide*** of 1769 remarked, 'The Market-place is very extensive and would form a beautiful Square, but for the Council-House which spoils the Figure. This is an old Gothic wooden building ...' Two contemporary observers, one of them an eye-witness to the fire, described the Council House as 'a miserable antiquated building' and 'a great desight [eyesore] to the market place'. A year afterwards, almost to the day, the Earl of Radnor offered to pay for a new council-house to be built. His condition, against the council's wishes, was that the new building should be raised in the centre of the Market Place. Eventually the matter was resolved when Bishop Barrington offered to demolish his guildhall to release the site for the construction of the new guildhall. His offer was accepted, work began in 1788 and the new building was opened in 1795.

At the time it might have appeared, with the resurgence of the cloth trade, and the developments of the previous half-century or so, that a bright destiny beckoned. But the clouds of war loomed. Revolution in France had resulted in the execution of the royal family and many leading figures in society and government and the establishment of a republic. In 1796 the British Government declared war on France, and over the ensuing 20 years, on any expression of radical politics at home. While the dean and chapter were raising the substantial sum of £300 for 'the defence of the kingdom', the city fathers were petitioning the king to sue for peace, claiming that the war was being 'carried on by an unexampled profusion of public money, and a system of delusion and corrupt influence, which threatens the subversion of the principles of our conduct.' How the city coped with the changes in society in the aftermath of war is the subject of the next chapter.

Chapter 7
'A fair old city' The 19th century

WHATEVER grounds for optimism there might have been in Salisbury at the start of the 19th century, prospects became ever more bleak as the conclusion of one war was succeeded within months by the outbreak of another.

The Collapse of the Cloth Trade

The impact of the Napoleonic War seems to have been wholly malign, as large parts of Europe which had provided Salisbury's textile manufacturers with their export markets fell within the hegemony of the First Empire, and were thus closed to those exports. The introduction of mechanisation proved to be a false dawn. Where it had been successful for hundreds of years was in the fulling mills, where water power was driving the machinery directly. To harness natural power to drive factory machinery required more power than was available in south Wiltshire: even in the north of England where such power levels were more generally available, these were supplemented through the use of atmospheric or steam pumps to recycle the driving water. The next phase of mechanisation was to apply steam power directly; but that required supplies of coal close to hand and a suitable means of transport, namely canals. Salisbury's competitors – the west of England towns producing wool, and the Lancashire towns producing cotton – enjoyed both of these advantages in abundance. So although mechanisation was attempted, it failed: the ***Salisbury Journal*** dated 20 July 1812 carries an advertisement for a steam engine bought only four years previously. The downward trend was already observable by 1805: the ***Triennial Directory*** of 1805 lists 31 traders in the textile trades, of whom 18 were clothiers: in Bradford the respective figures were 36 and 27, at Trowbridge 34 and 27. By 1814, Salisbury had only 13 clothiers, and by 1830 only three. Writing in 1843, Salisbury's historian, Henry Hatcher, dismissed the city's wares as 'too trifling to deserve notice'.

Agrarian Distress and the Swing Riots

The rural hinterland suffered equally severely, whether in consequence of the decline of cottage industries such as spinning, which supplied the city's shrinking needs, or of developments in agriculture and the impact of the wars. One result of the agrarian revolution of the late 18th and early 19th centuries was an increase in the size and efficiency of farms and a reduction in the need for labour. The ensuing depression in wages was made good by the Speenhamland system of outdoor relief which simply reduced the agricultural labourer to destitution, while the protection of the home market for cereals in the aftermath of the Napoleonic War through the Corn Laws put the basic necessities of life beyond the reach of many. First passed in 1815, they remained in force for 30 years and more. The resentments engendered by these conditions resulted in the Swing Riots, which raged throughout southern and eastern England from 1830 to 1832, and from which Salisbury was not immune.

Starting in Kent in August 1830, the disturbances reached Wiltshire in November. On the 23rd a mob bent on destroying Figes's iron foundry came into the city along the London Road and descended upon Colbourne's farm at Bishopdown to destroy his threshing machine. As the rioters reached the Green Croft they were intercepted by Wadham Wyndham, a magistrate with his posse of special constables, and the Salisbury troop of the Wiltshire Yeomanry. The Riot Act was read, but neither this nor the efforts of the consta-

Special Commission.

The MAYOR and JUSTICES beg to apprise their Fellow-Citizens, that the Special Commission, for the Trial of the Prisoners concerned in the late Riots, will be opened on Monday next, the 27th Inst., AND THAT ALL

SPECIAL CONSTABLES

Will be expected to render their ASSISTANCE in preserving the PEACE of the CITY, and securing all proper facilities to the Judges, Sheriff, Counsel, and others, during the progress of the Commission.

The SPECIAL CONSTABLES are desired to Assemble on MONDAY NEXT, at ONE O'CLOCK precisely, in their several Divisions, at the following Stations:

DIVISION A, at the WHITE HORSE INN, CASTLE-STREET.
B, at the BLACK HORSE INN.
C, in the CHEESE-MARKET.
DIVISION D, at the GOAT INN.
E, at the WHITE HART INN.
F, at the RADNOR ARMS.
G, at the RED LION INN.

BY ORDER OF THE MAYOR AND JUSTICES,

SALISBURY, Dec 22, 1830.

MATT. THOS. HODDING, Clerk.

Swing Riot posters. While some public notices (above) recruited special constables to maintain public order alongside the county yeomanry, others (below) exhorted would-be rioters to consider the cost to their livelihoods and their families.

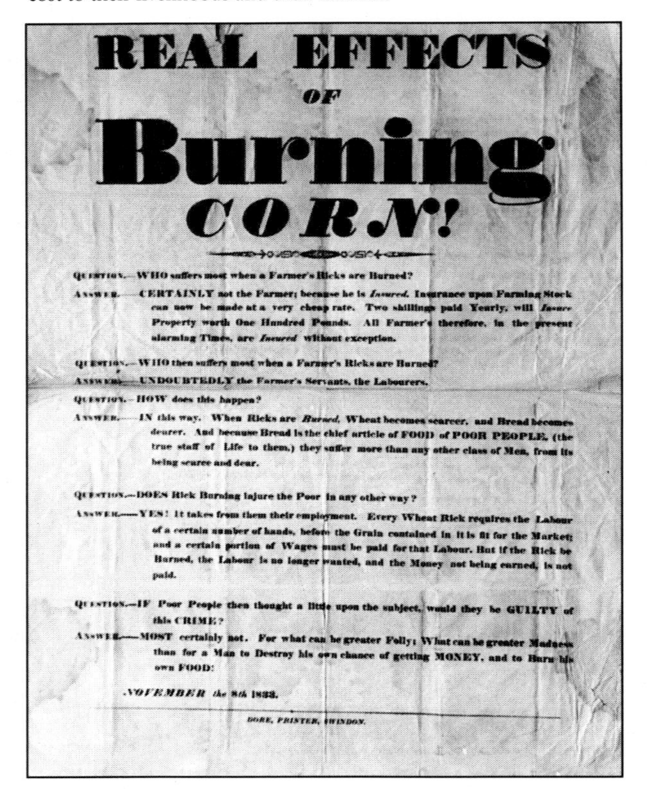

REAL EFFECTS OF Burning CORN!

QUESTION.—WHO suffers most when a Farmer's Ricks are Burned?

ANSWER.—CERTAINLY not the Farmer; because he is *Insured*. Insurance upon Farming Stock can now be made at a very cheap rate. Two shillings paid Yearly, will *Insure* Property worth One Hundred Pounds. All Farmer's therefore, in the present alarming Times, are *Insured* without exception.

QUESTION.—WHO then suffers most when a Farmer's Ricks are Burned?

ANSWER.—UNDOUBTEDLY the Farmer's Servants, the Labourers.

QUESTION.—HOW does this happen?

ANSWER.—IN this way. When Ricks are *Burned*, Wheat becomes scarcer, and Bread becomes *dearer*. And because Bread is the chief article of FOOD of POOR PEOPLE, (the true staff of Life to them,) they suffer more than any other class of Men, from its being scarce and dear.

QUESTION.—DOES Rick Burning injure the Poor in any other way?

ANSWER.—YES! It takes from them their employment. Every Wheat Rick requires the Labour of a certain number of hands, before the Grain contained in it is fit for the Market; and a certain portion of Wages must be paid for that Labour. But if the Rick be Burned, the Labour is no longer wanted, and the Money not being earned, is not paid.

QUESTION.—IF Poor People then thought a little upon the subject, would they be GUILTY of this CRIME?

ANSWER.—MOST certainly not. For what can be greater Folly; What can be greater Madness than for a Man to Destroy his own chance of getting MONEY, and to Burn his own FOOD:

NOVEMBER the 8th [illegible]

DORE, PRINTER, SWINDON.

bles to disperse the crowd had much effect, whereupon the Yeomanry charged. Twenty-two of the rioters were arrested and 17 were gaoled pending trial at a Special Assize held on 2 January 1831 to try the 339 charged for offences throughout the county. Facing the prisoners across the court as magistrate was John Benett of Pyt House, who was simultaneously the main prosecution witness and chairman of the jury. Although two Wiltshiremen condemned to death were reprieved, 150 were sentenced to transportation, 28 for life. As the riots subsided, there was relief in the countryside: wages were increased, and funds were provided for families to emigrate to a new life in the Antipodes.

Poor Relief

The city's solution to this economic distress was what it always had been: a mixture of savage repression in the courts, the work-house and a revival of initiatives similar to Ivie's two centuries earlier, one of which was clothed in a peculiarly 19th-century reaction to destitution, the Society for the Suppression of Mendicity, founded in 1818. The perception lying behind this organisation was that those reduced to beggary diverted almsgiving from more worthy causes, and were carriers of the disease which still stalked the city. The solution lay in opening two lodging houses in Culver Street and St Ann Street, accessible only by vouchers: they were still in operation in 1840, and providing 5,000 admissions per year. However, the scheme, which relied partly on private beneficence and partly on parish funds, was brought suddenly to an end when support from the parishes was withdrawn. Another approach to the relief of hardship was to set up a silk mill in Castle Street in succession to Senescal's mill, which had closed in 1825. It gave employment to over 100 people for some years, but its later history and ultimate fate are unknown.

Meanwhile, the workhouse, never short of customers, attracted sharp criticism from the Poor Law Commissioners in 1834, who reported that they had never experienced '...a more disgusting scene of filth and misrule than the Salisbury workhouse'. The solution lay in the establishment, under the Poor Law Amendment Act, of unions of parishes, to pool resources to provide a system of indoor relief, approximately uniform across the country. However, the Salisbury Union continued to use the Crane Street workhouse until 1879. The new Alderbury Union was set up in 1836, serving the Liberty of the Close and the parishes to the south and east of the city, and housing 200 inmates with savings on the poor rates. The two unions combined in 1868, and a new workhouse was built in 1879 on the site of the old Alderbury Union workhouse just south of the city. A reminder of just

The Parishes of St. Thomas, St. Edmund and St. Martin, New Sarum.

To the Churchwardens and Overseers of the Poor of the respective Parishes of Saint Thomas, Saint Edmund and Saint Martin, in the City of New Sarum, in the County of Wilts.

To the Clerk or Clerks to the Justices of the Petty Sessions held for the Division or Divisions in which the said Parishes are situate; —and to all others whom it may concern.

WE, THE POOR LAW COMMISSIONERS, in pursuance of the Authorities vested in Us by an Act passed in the fifth Year of the Reign of His late Majesty King WILLIAM the Fourth, intituled "*An Act for the Amendment and better Administration of the Laws relating to the Poor in England and Wales*," Do hereby Order and Declare, that the Rules, Orders, and Regulations herein contained relating to the government of the Workhouse belonging to the Parishes of Saint Thomas, Saint Edmund and Saint Martin, in the City of New Sarum, in the County of Wilts, shall, after the expiration of twenty-one days from the date hereof, be observed and become imperative and binding on the parties concerned.

And We do hereby Declare that any of the authorities hereby conferred on the said Parties may thenceforth be exercised by them.

The original Salisbury Union: the charge from the Commissioners. This document enjoined the overseers of the city parishes to form the Salisbury Union, in accordance with the Poor Law Amendment Act of 1834, and to adopt and apply the ensuing code of rules for the running of the workhouse.

how harsh workhouse life was can be gauged from the punishment for disorderly behaviour, which included playing cards 'or at any other game of chance': 'substituting, during a time not greater than 48 hours, for … dinner … a meal consisting of eight ounces of bread, or one pound of cooked potatoes, and also by withholding from him during the same period, all butter, cheese, tea, sugar or broth, which such pauper would otherwise receive, at any meal during the time aforesaid.' Gradually conditions improved, partly as a result of local initiatives and responses to local problems, partly as a result of the great swathe of political, social and economic reforms undertaken by the governments of the 1830s and 1840s. At the same time there was something of a change in the spirit of the age: Hatcher remarked of his own time that the 'habit of tippling' had disappeared, and the prevailing ethos resulted in two famous coaching inns, the George and the Three Swans, becoming temperance and family hotels.

One of the last major reforms of the old city council was the provision of street lighting by gas following the founding of the Salisbury Gas Company in 1832. The gasworks lay just to the north of the junction of Wilton and Devizes Roads: understandably the first street to be lit was Fisherton Street in 1833, with lighting spreading rapidly eastwards thereafter. It was, however, several decades before gas was to be used widely for domestic lighting and cooking. Electric power, like gas initially produced to provide lighting, came to Salisbury in 1899.

Municipal Reform

The Great Reform Act of 1832, sweeping away the tourist attraction of Old Sarum among all the other rotten boroughs, is probably the most readily recalled of all the reforming measures of the 1830s and 1840s. What is of as much significance is that the franchise within the city itself was greatly extended, from the 58 councillors to the householders whose properties were rated at £10 annually. The franchise was still far beyond the grasp of working men, let alone women, but the political process was opened up to a far broader range of thought and opinion than previously: W.B. Brodie, editor of the ***Salisbury Journal*** and an ardent advocate of reform, had polled only seven votes in the 1831 Parliamentary election; in that of 1833 he topped the poll. As important for the future of the city was the passage of the Municipal Corporations Act of 1835. The corporation which came into being on 1 January 1836 comprised the mayor, six aldermen and 18 councillors, elected by ratepayers of the three wards and living within seven miles, and the area governed by the council corresponded with the Parliamentary Borough, taking in the built up areas of the parishes of Fisherton and Milford, and the liberty of the Close. With the exception of replacing the high constables and sub-constables with a proper, salaried, police force, the activities of the new corporation were not, initially, very different from the old. The curious separation of powers remained whereby the Overseers of the Poor retained control of poor relief, and the Directors of Highways the condition of the streets – and thereby the watercourses.

Jeux Video
Neufs
Occasions
Meubles

Cholera

It took a combination of independent professional opinion, the passing of the Public Health Act in 1848 and a final, devastating epidemic to force the corporation to adopt the act in 1852 and to embark on the filling in of the open watercourses and the Town Ditch, and the provision of proper sewerage and water supplies. Before the outbreak of cholera in 1849 opinion was sharply divided as to the merits of the watercourses, the issue having come to the fore when the city was surveyed in 1845 by an inspector for the Health of Towns Commission. That report concluded that although there was a serious public health problem arising from lack of sanitation, the worst affected areas within the city were the courtyards within the chequers, which, because they had no frontage onto the streets and were not served by the watercourses, were not a concern the Directors of Highways had any power to address.

Cholera reached Salisbury in July 1849. The first death was recorded on 8 July, and the epidemic continued for two months, carrying off 192 people, over two per cent of the city's population. Although this was nowhere near the mortality rate from the plague of 1627, which was over 12 per cent, the figure was sufficiently high to persuade the editor of the ***Salisbury Journal*** to impose an embargo on the subject, for fear of fomenting alarm and despondency, until the epidemic was on the wane; there were, besides, more than 1,300 admissions to the Infirmary for cholera, and several dozen deaths from causes connected with it.

A variety of solutions were proposed. John Winzar, medical officer to the Overseers of the Poor, suggested the watercourses be retained, asserting that 'Neither nature nor art could possibly have formed channels better adapted for carrying away the sewage of the city'. Another proposal was for the retention of the watercourses for water supply and to serve as sweet-water drains, and the construction of a separate system of foul drains. The idea of dispensing with the watercourses altogether and providing separate systems for water supply and sewage was advocated only by a minority, and in the aftermath of the epidemic, the Directors of Highways attempted to improve matters by re-opening the watercourses and clearing them of accumulated refuse, and by jerry-building a drainage system in the north-east of the city. The leading reformer, Andrew Middleton, had already observed the unpalatable fact that sewage was disposed of by cesspits which contaminated the city's wells, or by discharge from drains into the watercourses, and he had no doubt of the connection between cholera and the contamination of water supplies. He therefore petitioned the General Board of Health to survey the city's sanitary arrangements, and although his 60 petitioners were far outnumbered by a counter-petition representing vested interests, the

A section of the Close Ditch. In this section, recently excavated during some foundation repairs in Church House, John Carley, diocesan surveyor, shows that at this point the ditch was about 6ft wide.

London Road Cemetery, from Roe's ***Illustrations*** of *c.*1860. This view from the top of the cemetery down to the London Road dates from only a few years after the opening of the cemetery: hence its open aspect. The Nonconformist chapel is on the left, the Anglican chapel is on the right.

(Left) Watercourse in Rouen. Had they been allowed to remain, Salisbury's watercourses would have looked much like this example in Rouen, and doubtless would have been seen as an inconvenience.

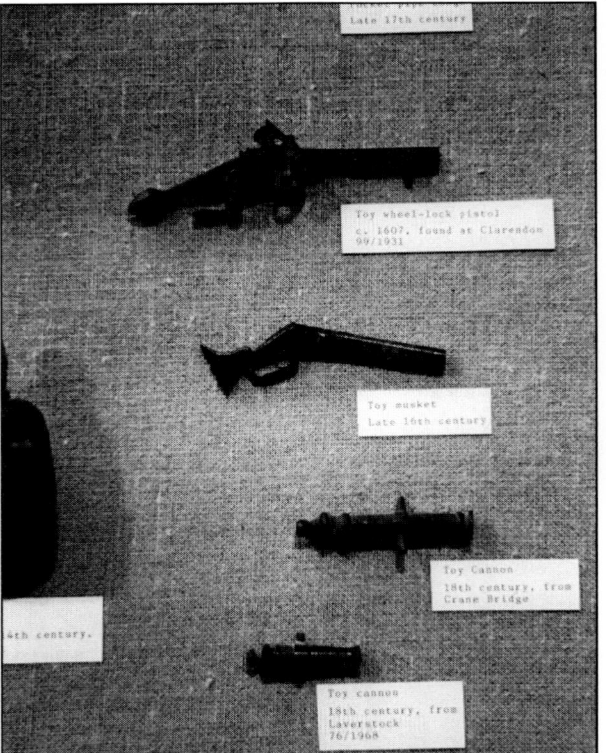

Artefacts from the watercourses. The founding collection for the Salisbury and South Wiltshire Museum was known as the Drainage Collection, and the artefacts shown here, recovered from the drains as they were cleared, include (top) keys, (above) pilgrim's badges depicting St Thomas of Canterbury and (left) toy guns from various locations.

board had the power to send in an inspector because the death rate was in excess of 23 per 1,000. The independent professional opinion was voiced in a report compiled by Thomas Webster Rammell: he endorsed Middleton's findings and roundly condemned the directors' vain attempts to forestall more radical action with their recently-built and ill-considered drainage system.

Thus the city was compelled to adopt the Act, and over the following decades a modern water supply and sewage system was installed throughout the city. By September 1854 Salisbury had a pure water supply, and deep sewers which carried effluent away into the Avon, and over the next six years city properties were connected to these systems, while simultaneously the street channels were filled in, concluding with the Close Ditch in 1860. Finally, in 1875 the Town Ditch in New Canal was filled in. From 1885, sewage was partially treated at Bugmore before discharge into the Avon, and from 1899 improvements were made which enabled the Bugmore sewage farm to serve the city until 1961.

Might the watercourses have survived? They could have been retained as surface water drainage, and the effect would have been similar to that in the old quarter of Rouen or King's Parade in Cambridge. Whether they would have survived the coming of the motor car is another matter entirely.

Two other products of the public health reforms at this time were the building of the municipal cemeteries away from the city centre, on the Devizes and London Roads, and, following the adoption of the Baths and Washhouses Act of 1846, the city's first public bath was provided, by the Avon, near to what today is Market Walk, in 1875. There were two other consequences unlooked for at the time, but of inestimable value to historians. One was the recovery from the watercourses of enormous quantities of the products of Salisbury craftsmanship from the earliest times. These objects were auctioned in 1859 for £32 10s, and formed the core of the collection at the Salisbury and South Wiltshire Museum, opened at No.1 Castle Street in 1861 by Dr Richard Fowler. The other was the mapping of the city by the surveyors Kingdon and Shearm of Launceston, at the scale of 1:528 (10ft to 1 mile) in 1854 to plot the lines of the sewers, providing an invaluable snapshot of the city in the years before the arrival of the railway in Fisherton.

The Arrival of the Railways and the Death of the Stage-coach

The railways came relatively late to Salisbury, commencing with a standard-gauge line from Salisbury to Bishopstoke – the village whose hamlet of Eastleigh was to become Hampshire's railway town – and thence to London. Initially opened for goods traffic on 27 January 1847, the railway began carrying passengers on 1 March. It was another defining moment in Salisbury's history, because it was not long before London was within a day's return journey, and the railway brought the outside world that much more within Salisbury's reach, and Salisbury within the world's grasp. The occasion of the railway's arrival in 1847 was marked with a banquet at the White Hart Hotel, where one of the speakers expressed the aspiration of Salisbury's becoming the 'Manchester of the South', which, given the lack of industrial infrastructure by that time, was probably a vain hope, although there can be no

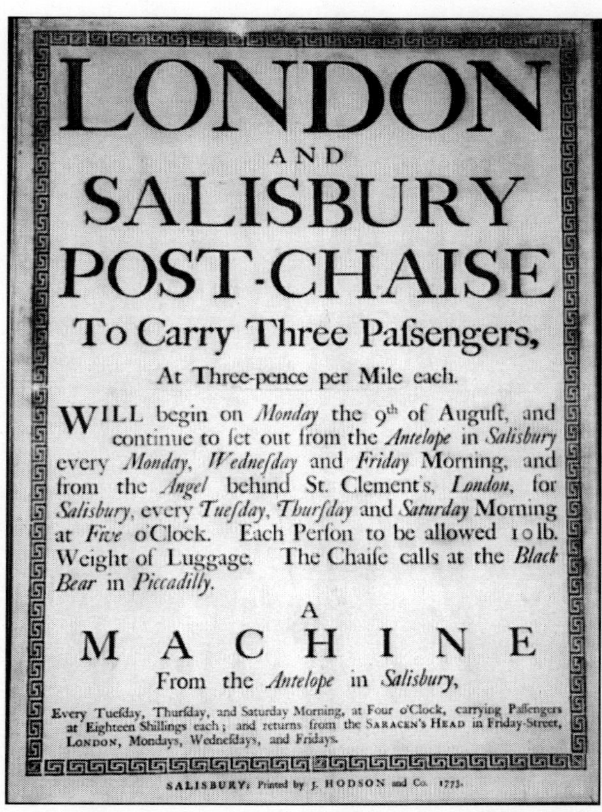

LONDON
AND
SALISBURY
POST-CHAISE
To Carry Three Pafsengers,
At Three-pence per Mile each.

WILL begin on *Monday* the 9th of Auguft, and continue to fet out from the *Antelope* in *Salisbury* every *Monday*, *Wednefday* and *Friday* Morning, and from the *Angel* behind St. Clement's, *London*, for *Salisbury*, every *Tuefday*, *Thurfday* and *Saturday* Morning at *Five* o'Clock. Each Perfon to be allowed 10 lb. Weight of Luggage. The Chaife calls at the *Black Bear* in *Piccadilly*.

A
MACHINE
From the *Antelope* in *Salisbury*,

Every Tuefday, Thurfday, and Saturday Morning, at Four o'Clock, carrying Paffengers at Eighteen Shillings each; and returns from the SARACEN'S HEAD in Friday-Street, LONDON, Mondays, Wednefdays, and Fridays.

SALISBURY: Printed by J. HODSON and Co. 1773.

Post-chaise poster. This poster, detailing departure and arrival times and fares, shows just how slow and expensive public transport was at a time when there really was no alternative.

The 1856 accident at the GWR terminus at Fisherton. One of two contemporary watercolours, both of which emphasise the darkness, the pandemonium and the stench of suffering and death.

doubting the railway's role in shaping the city as it is today.

Nevertheless, it was to be almost a decade before Salisbury would be accessible from the west, commencing with the Great Western Railway's line from Bristol via Warminster, opening on 30 June 1856. This was followed by the competing line from London via Basingstoke and Andover in 1857, of which the westward extension to Gillingham and on, by 1860, to Exeter, necessitated the construction of a separate station at Fisherton. The effects on the transport system and on the life of the city were dramatic. At the start of the 19th century, there were 10 stage-coaches, as well as the Mail, travelling to London, offering 52 services each week. At their height, in 1839, coaches provided 59 services to London each week, carrying over 50,000 passengers in the year; Bath and Southampton were served by 31 and 40 services respectively each week. However, travel was slow and expensive: the rate per mile varied between 2d for outside passengers and 5d inside, the 'Machine' which left the Antelope Inn for London cost 18s for the single journey, and the journey time was at least nine hours: even in 1830 there were some services taking up to 16 hours. By contrast, on the railways even the indirect route to London via Bishopstoke took only four hours, and the first direct service took three-and-a-half hours. The return fares were initially 24s first class and 18s 6d second class, but by 1850 an excursion to London cost just 3s 6d. By 1857, the service to London could take as little as three hours and eight minutes – for first and second-class passengers; the third-class journey took two hours longer.

The coaching industry survived only by providing connecting services to main line stations: in the case of the London line, from Salisbury to the Andover Road station. The impact of the railways was such that the Quicksilver plied its last run to London in October 1846, four months before the first rail passenger service. Alongside progress there was an early portent of disaster when on Monday 6 October 1856, just four months after the line from Warminster was opened, a livestock train drawn by two engines overshot the terminus buffers. Driver Nicholas and fireman Eyles of the second engine were the only human casualties: over 100 sheep, most of the consignment, were killed or seriously injured, the latter being dispatched by the slaugh-

Market House from Roe's ***Illustrations of Salisbury*** *c.*1860.

termen of two local butchers, Edward Judd and Thomas Dowding. The service to the city was completed in 1859, when Britain's shortest standard gauge railway was inaugurated, to link the station with the Market House, opened on 24 May that year.

At the Market House there were weekly sales of grain, leading to the building becoming known as the Corn Market, monthly sales of cheese and an annual wool sale. Despite its symbolism of Victorian affluence, the Market House suffered somewhat mixed fortunes, as, although the corn market continued until the end of the building's commercial life, the monthly cheese and annual wool markets had lapsed before World War Two. The railway which had run as far as the end of the present Market Walk was closed in 1918, and the line provided transport for the maltings and for bringing coal to the nearby Town Mill when its electric generating capacity was converted from water to steam power fired by coal. The Market House was used as a venue for a wide variety of events – pet shows, dinners, concerts and political meetings, professional wrestling and badminton. It was also leased to the Wiltshire Rifle Volunteers and subsequently the Wiltshire County Territorial Association as a drill hall and meeting place.

The Exhibition of 1852

There were other, more transient but no less telling manifestations of Salisbury's prosperity. In 1852, echoing the Great Exhibition of 1851, there was held in the Guildhall 'The Salisbury Exhibition of Local Industry, Amateur Productions, Works of Art, Antiquities, Objects of Taste, Articles of Vertu, etc.' There were 88 trade exhibitors, whose wares were displayed in the Council Chamber, the Law Court and the Hall, and of these 49 included the products of local industry. The range of manufactures was enormous, from cork to edged and other tools, to tobacco pipes and paper decorations, and from calotype photographs to prize-winning twines and cords, to dog-cart wheels. There were ammonites from Lyme Regis, there was tobacco grown in Salisbury, there was a Chinese Pagoda

Tiffin lithograph of the Exhibition. Displays were mounted in the Law Court and the Banqueting Hall and the exhibition is known to have been visited by over 7,000 people. The view above is of the Law Court.

Tiffin lithograph of the Banqueting Hall display of the Salisbury Exhibition. One of the stands is for Edward Roe, whose illustrations appear on pages 81 aand 84.

assembled from 4,500 pieces of elder pith, cases of 'dental surgery' and of moths, and two models of Stonehenge. Had one wished to see local textiles, there was lace from Downton and Redlynch, and a 'Specimen of the finest Black Cloth manufactured in Wiltshire'; but the shawls were from Lyons and Edinburgh, the damasks from Ireland, Scotland and Barnsley, and the flannels from Saxony.

Occupations in the Later 19th Century

This multiplicity of occupations can be seen in contemporary directories of trades and professions. By 1880, a generation after the 1852 exhibition, Salisbury had its own bird stuffer, as much a reflection of a demand for the preservation of hunting trophies as of an interest in natural history, alongside collections of fossils and lepidoptera. There was also a cork-cutter who served the needs of the local brewing industry and dispensing chemists as well as home wine and cordial makers. There were two cycle manufacturers, one of whom also made sewing machines. There were many traders whose businesses covered a spectrum of activities, sometimes related – like James Lush, a corn dealer and sack contractor, or Arthur Foley, wholesale and retail cabinet maker, upholsterer, paperhanger and carpet warehouseman, and sometimes apparently not, like Mrs Martha Bailey, toy dealer and perfumer.

The role of women in business is one of the most interesting aspects of the economic history of the city. Among those who were married or perhaps widowed there were, unsurprisingly, seven shopkeepers and three who maintained registers of servants; there were milliners, a straw bonnet maker, and a hatter and furrier. But there were also an umbrella maker, a builder, three corn dealers, two boot and shoe makers, two plumbers, one of whom was also a glazier, a photographer, a tobacconist, and Sarah Judd, widow of the aforementioned butcher Edward Judd. Among the unmarried, there were the seven dressmakers, the tailor

J.W. Lovibond, brewer, inventor of the Tintometer system of comparative colorimetry and Mayor of Salisbury 1877–78 and 1889–90.

and the three milliners, but there was also a pianoforte and music seller. There are numerous instances of schoolmistresses, several of whom run substantial businesses, and there are several examples of partnerships and companies, running anything from Berlin wool shops, to schools, to hat manufacture. In light of this considerable stake in the city's prosperity it is not surprising that women were active in local politics, unmarried women ratepayers being enfranchised in municipal elections from 1867.

Among the businesses for which in the late Victorian era Salisbury was famous, the Invicta Leather Works, founded in 1824 in Endless Street, was noted, by 1897, as being 'one of the chief industrial centres in Salisbury, and the largest leather currying business in the West of England, over 100 hands finding constant employment in the varying departments of the business'. It survived until 1971 as Colonia (Sarum) Ltd, by specialising in dressing reptile skins. More distinctive and more enduring is The Tintometer Ltd, which arose from the activities of the brewer Joseph Lovibond, who devised a system of assaying his product by reference to coloured glass slides. The system could be applied reliably to any chemical product which is transparent in solution and could thus be marketed throughout the industry.

With rare exceptions, such as power generation, brewing and the leather works mentioned above, Salisbury never developed any large-scale productive industry in the late 19th century. The growth areas in employment which took up the increase in the city's population, which more than doubled in the 19th century from 7,668 to 17,117, were in the service industries – schools, hospitals, the railways. In 1899 there were 10 national and church schools, and a further 10 independent schools, five each for boys and girls. There were five colleges, including the Theological College, the Diocesan Training College for National Schoolmistresses and the School of Science and Art. The Fisherton House Lunatic Asylum was the largest private lunatic asylum in the country. Mass tourism began with the development of the railways, and was augmented when the Army became a major economic force in the county from the late 19th century onwards with the development of the Salisbury Plain Training Area. The plain was first used for the large formation exercises known as manoeuvres by the Army in 1872, culminating with a royal review of the troops on 12 September of that year at Bulford. The need for manoeuvres and target practice over a distance once rifles were developed with a range in excess of 1,000 yards prompted the purchase of some 40,000 acres at £10 per acre. The training area extended roughly from Shrewton and Bulford in the south to West Lavington and Everleigh in the north, while today's training area occupies some 92,000 acres.

The Housing Boom of the Late 19th Century

This growth is reflected in the housing boom which Salisbury experienced throughout the 19th century, whether in and around Fisherton Anger or between Castle Road and the London Road. Fisherton had begun as a village with its main street on a north-south axis, with its church on that street. As it developed in the 17th century as a suburb of Salisbury, specialising in accommodation for travellers to and from the west, the road towards Wilton became its main thoroughfare. With the arrival of the gasworks and the railway there developed two distinct quarters, to the south and to the

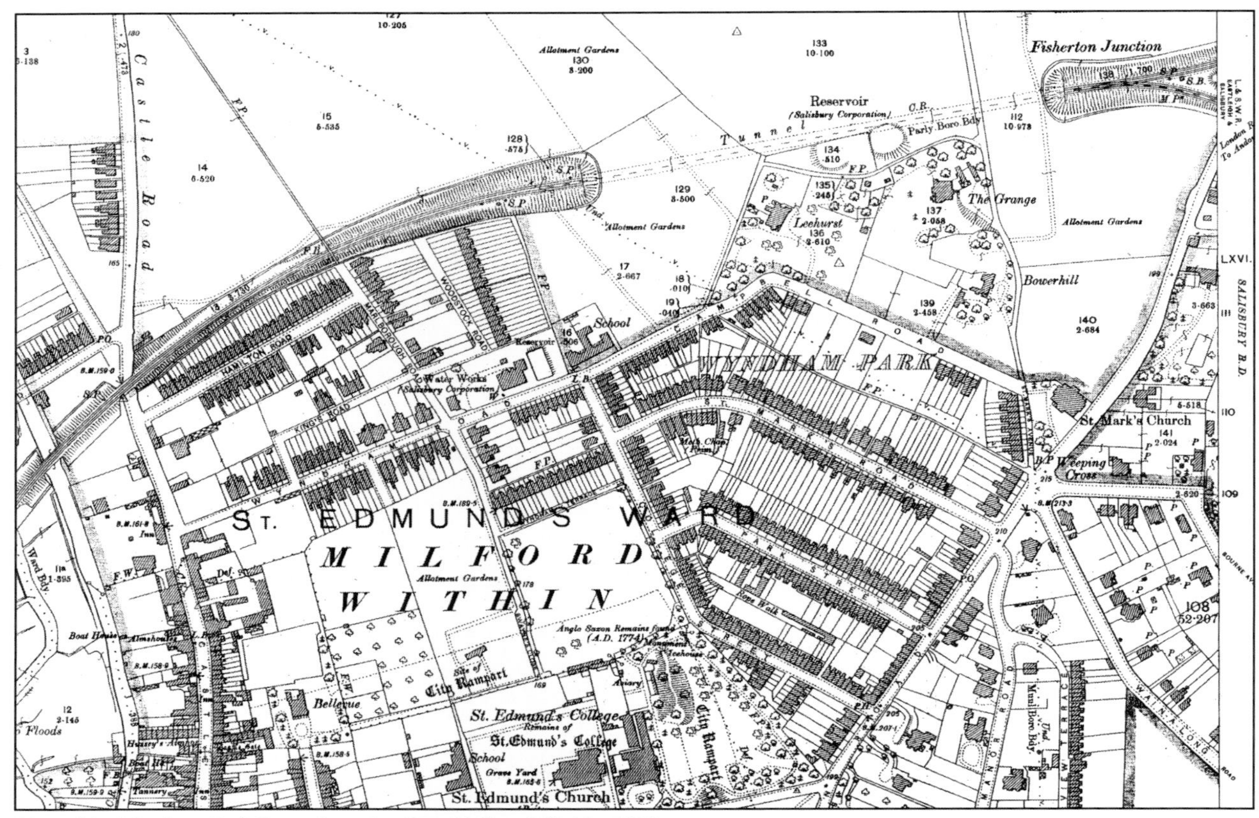

Map of the Wyndham Park Estate, from the 1901 OS Sheet Wiltshire LXVI.11.

north of Fisherton Street. A third quarter developed either side of the Wilton Road, of slightly more upmarket properties, from around 1860 onwards. In the city proper, and to the east, the main areas of development were, to the south, the Friary and the area around St Martin's Church and the Milford railway terminus; the area around Milford Hill and east of the Greencroft; and the grounds of The College, the city home of the Wyndham family. This latter was sold in 1871, and the resulting housing, from the last quarter of the 19th century, is typical 'bye-law' housing, the street-plan allowing for two terraces of houses with narrow frontages, rooms one behind the other and long, strip-like back gardens leading to an alleyway running through the centre of the plot. The 1891 Census returns and contemporary directories show who lived in these houses when they were new: two saddle and harness makers, two policemen, a piano tuner, a boot closer, a bank clerk, a railway signalman, a boot and shoe pattern cutter, a postal telegraphist and the manager of the Turkish Baths in Queen Street; most if not all of whom came from the city or the surrounding area. The contrast with those who could afford the villas in nearby Manor, London and Campbell Roads is striking. Here lived two clerks in holy orders and a Baptist minister, a bank sub-manager, two solicitors, a land agent and a retired merchant: they hailed from as far afield as Cornwall and Kent, Lincolnshire and Suffolk, but none from Salisbury. Between them the two groups provide a foretaste of Salisbury's social make-up in the next century.

'Bye-law' housing, Hamilton Road.

Chapter 8

'The apple of the eye of England' – Newer Sarum – the 20th century

TRANSPORT, Salisbury's lifeblood in the railway era, had threatened to become its nemesis with the first accident occurring only months after the opening of the Great Western line. In the 20th century after World War One, transport was to continue to bring life and vigour to the city, and to threaten a rather different form of nemesis. But that earlier form – the sudden and catastrophic loss of life – was to strike the city from three directions in the earliest decades.

The 1906 Rail Disaster and Afterwards

The first blow fell on 1 July 1906, when the boat train from Plymouth carrying mainly American passengers who had arrived on the SS ***New York*** travelled through the station at speed. Increasing competition had driven journey times down – the Salisbury-London journey time had been cut by more than half in 50 years – and the timetable for this service to Waterloo was 4 hours 20 minutes. At the station the line has an extremely tight

The 1906 rail disaster. In contrast to that of 50 years earlier, the scene of the 1906 accident was extensively recorded, and photographs were disseminated widely as supplements in the national press and as postcards.

The 1906 rail disaster.

A tank on its tour of the city crosses from Catherine Street into St John's Street, on 5 March 1918, during War Bond Week. The initial appeal was for £52,500, enough to buy a fleet of 21 aeroplanes. As the tally exceeded double that amount, it was proudly announced in the press that funds were sufficient for the aeroplanes and a fleet of 10 tanks at £5,000 apiece.

(Above) The War Memorial, unveiled by Lt Adlam on 12 February 1922. Behind is the statue of Sidney Herbert (Baron Herbert of Lea), later removed to Victoria Park. (Below) The War Memorial, 2002, including a memorial plaque to the fallen of World War Two.

curve – one arc of an S-bend – with a speed limit of 35mph. But the express train was estimated to be travelling at a mile a minute, and the lateral forces drove it off the rails and against the milk train on the down line, and another, stationary engine. In the ensuing mayhem 28 were killed and 11 hurt, including 24 and seven respectively of the 43 passengers. The Infirmary received a letter of thanks from President Roosevelt for its care of his injured countrymen, and for years afterwards trains were forced to halt on the approach to the station.

When disaster again struck within six years, it was the city's turn to mourn, for five lives were lost in the sinking of the ***Titanic.***

The impact of World War One was felt in a number of ways. There were, of course, the appeals to patriotism: a recruiting office was set up in what is now the HSBC's premises on the corner of Minster Street and the Market Place. The Infirmary cared for almost 3,000 troops, and there were regular notices in the local press asking for books for convalescing soldiers. There were also advertisements for the 'Chemico' body protector – a bullet-proof vest – and trench-coats, and news of fund-raising for such home comforts on the Front as 10,000 cigarettes. Advertisements for Pears' soap carried the postscript, 'don't forget to send the boy some in the next parcel'. In addition there were appeals to women to aid the war effort by joining the Land Army, and for materiel, including tanks and aircraft. Funds for these were raised in the War Bond Weeks: in 1918, the target for the week, from 4–10 March, was £52,500, enough to buy a fleet of 21 aeroplanes. A tank was brought along to tour the streets on the Tuesday and Wednesday, accompanied by the Giant and Hob-Nob. The Salisbury Company of Volunteers subscribed over £4,000, and the total raised by the city reached £165,204. When women secured the vote in 1918, the local campaign against women's suffrage, spearheaded by Lady Hulse and Lady Radnor, made over its funds to the war effort. News of the war was carried in the press, while the new medium of the cinema was enlisted in support of morale and information. In one week in April 1916 there was the choice of 'With the RFC at the Front' at the Palace in Endless Street, and 'Britain prepared – the big topical film' at the New Theatre in Castle Street.

The city's death toll in World War One was 459. Salisbury's returning hero was Lt Tom Edwin Adlam, who was awarded the Victoria Cross for bravery during the Battle of the Somme. On 27 and 28 September, at roughly the mid-point of the battle, with the village of Thiepval as the objective, Adlam advanced, gathering troops and enemy hand-grenades in order to attack pockets of enemy resistance. Before the war, he had been a schoolmaster, and had developed the skill of throwing cricket balls, with which knack and the grenades, he cleared the German positions. He was twice wounded, but with his troops he gained 300 yards, and his efforts contributed substantially to the capture of the Schwaben Redoubt. On his award the pupils at his school, St Martin's, were given a half-holiday. In 1922, after Earl Haig had declined the invitation, he unveiled the War Memorial. The war changed the world for ever, and Salisbury was not immune from those changes. Industry, particularly mechanical engineering, was disrupted by the demands of the war effort.

The Scout Motor Car

An example of Edwardian enterprise which fell victim to World War One was the range of vehicles designed by the Scout Motor Company. The origins of the business lay in the firm of Burden Brothers, manufacturers of church and turret clocks in Fisherton and, from 1899, on the Southampton (now Tollgate) Road. While there the firm diversified into the manufacture of internal combustion engines, and by 1903 had moved into new premises in the Friary, to begin making motorcycles and motorboats and to design the first car, which was registered in September 1905. The workforce, some 75 strong, earned from 10s 5d to £1 11s 3d for a 50-hour week and each car could take up to eight weeks to build. The custom during 1906 of distinguished clients, coupled with success in engine trials and the 1906 Isle of Man Tourist Race, swelled the order books, and prompted the move to Churchfields, in Bemerton. By 1909 the product range comprised six cars and five commercial vehicles. The firm's peak production was

Scout car. The 6-cylinder 30-hp 'Roi des Belges' model of 1908, with Scout's test driver William Lucas at the wheel. Like most cars of the period, the car has an open tourer body; the drivetrain and chassis were built by Scout's, and the bodies by Farr's, another local firm.

attained in 1912, with 150 on the payroll and two vehicles built each week. In that year they embarked upon the manufacture of commercial vehicles – ambulances, buses and charabancs – and thereby contributed to the development of motor bus services connecting surrounding villages with Salisbury.

However, a combination of wartime government decisions and post-war economic conditions led to the firm's collapse. Firstly, the plant was commandeered in 1915 for manufacturing operations in France, and production at Bemerton was switched to ordnance. Not until early 1920 could vehicle manufacture resume: by then the company had to contend both with enormously increased labour and materials costs, and competition from the likes of Fiat, Ford and Morris. With its wide range of models and Burden's insistence on manufacture of components great and small, the product range was simply too expensive, and the firm was wound up in June 1921. Had more components been outsourced (as was common practice in the cycle industry, whence Rover had arisen) and had fewer designs been adapted to a variety of functions (as pioneered by Ford) the history of the Scout and Salisbury's destiny might have been very different.

Economic Development since 1918

With the failure of Scout Motors Ltd passed a major opportunity for large-scale industrial development, and the threat of unemployment loomed as troops returned. Simultaneously there was a housing shortage, as there had been no building during the war, and the population had risen from 21,217 in 1911 to 22,861 in 1921. The solution had already been considered during the war, for local authorities had been empowered since 1875 by the Artisans' Dwellings Act and later legislation to undertake social housing. Land was acquired by the city for council housing off the Devizes Road in March 1919, and more shortly afterwards off Wain-a-long Road. The cost of building was partly met by the issue of housing bonds from August 1920, and in September the project was launched with a stone-laying ceremony in Macklin Road. A year later, 42 houses had been built, as were others as part of a mixed development at Netherhampton. The Wain-a-long Road development followed in 1924, as did the Waters Road Estate, between the Stratford and Castle Roads. In 1929 and 1930 another estate was built, comprising Butts Road, Douglas Haig Road and part of Hulse Road.

In addition to providing much-needed housing, the schemes provided employment throughout the 1920s. Following the stock market crash of 1929 there was a serious recession throughout the 1930s, and Arthur Maidment remarked on seeing dole queues in Catherine Street 'three or four men deep the length of the street'. Gradually, the economy recovered and new industries arrived to absorb the unemployed. In 1920, for example, there were 22 businesses in the motor trade: by 1939 there were 52, including three tyre factors, a driving school and a motor damage assessor. In 1920, Salisbury had one haulage contractor, in 1939, eight; over the same period the builders had increased from four firms to 10. Extensive private housing was erected between the Castle and London Roads on land which had been earmarked for a new general hospital: the streets were named after wards in the Infirmary. What would nowadays be called sunrise industries, reflecting changes in commerce and lifestyle, had developed from scratch by 1939: these included office equipment suppliers, electrical engineers (four each), perambulator manufacturers (two), wireless engineers (nine), turf commission agents (five) and a teacher of elocution. National enterprises with offices in Salisbury included the Anglo-American Oil Company, British Sugar Corporation, Elders and Fyffes, Hoovers, Roads Reconstruction Ltd and Walls.

World War Two and After

The outbreak of war in 1939 had a number of consequences for Salisbury. In common with other towns and cities deemed safe from enemy attack, Salisbury received its quota of evacuees – almost 2,500 children and their teachers, from the Portsmouth area. Yet despite the Town Clerk's misgivings on account of the presence of the military in various guises all around the city, and Southampton, a prime target, only minutes away, Salisbury was attacked by the Luftwaffe on only a handful of occasions. During two night raids in June 1940, high explosive and incendiary bombs were dropped, the latter causing some damage to property. A Messerschmitt Me110 strafed a convoy on the London Road in July 1940; then in August 1942, the city was attacked twice within a few days. On the 11th a pair of

Focke-Wulf FW190 fighters flew down Castle Street and attacked the Gas Works and the railway line; on the 14th a Heinkel He111 flew along Fisherton Street, its pilot intent on attacking the railway with gunfire and bombs. As in 1940, there was damage to property (including the demolition of the mayor's house) but by great good fortune no loss of life.

However, the war had the effect of further strengthening the city's economy, by bringing industries scattered by enemy action into the city. Among these were the aircraft manufacturer Supermarine, which came to Castle Road to build Spitfires when it became clear that Southampton could expect bombing raids. Another wartime visitor which remained in Salisbury until 2000 was Wellworthy, the piston ring manufacturer, latterly A.E. Goetze. Indeed, manufacturing industry in Salisbury has tended to be light engineering, with a slant towards high technology and specialised sectors or niche markets. Firms include Pains-Wessex (pyrotechnics), Janspeed (motor tuning specialists) and Naim (high-quality audio equipment), and are concentrated in four main areas – adjacent to Hudson's Field and at Old Sarum, to the north of the city, and along the Southampton Road and at the Churchfields Industrial Estate to the south. One recent casualty was the innovative Edgeley Optica light aeroplane, built at Old Sarum from 1985 to 1990. Another was the Rural Development Commission, formerly the Council for Small Industries in Rural Areas, whose aims were particularly apposite in view of Salisbury's industry, and whose objectives included advice, specialist publications and training workshops which met needs not catered for by other training agencies.

The building of post-war housing has continued apace, as the city's population has increased from 26,140 in 1931, to 33,079 in 1951, to 36,840 in 1991. 1950s private developments, principally in Laverstock and the Paul's Dene area, were matched by a mixed development on Bishopdown, and the council development on Bemerton Heath. This latter was famed for its provision of hot water from a central boiler, from the late 1940s to the mid-1950s, which a former resident, Chris Usher, recalls as being extremely efficient. More recent developments have been on the site of the Harvard Hospital, built and run by the American military during the last war, and the Bishopdown Farm estate, approved in 1994 and still in progress.

Planning Issues and the By-Pass

Salisbury's key position in the south's rail network; as a growing centre of population (estimates for 1996 and the present time are 41,900 and 42,700 respectively); as a market centre; and as a tourist attraction have had important implications for transport management. The passage of the Town and Country Planning Act of 1949

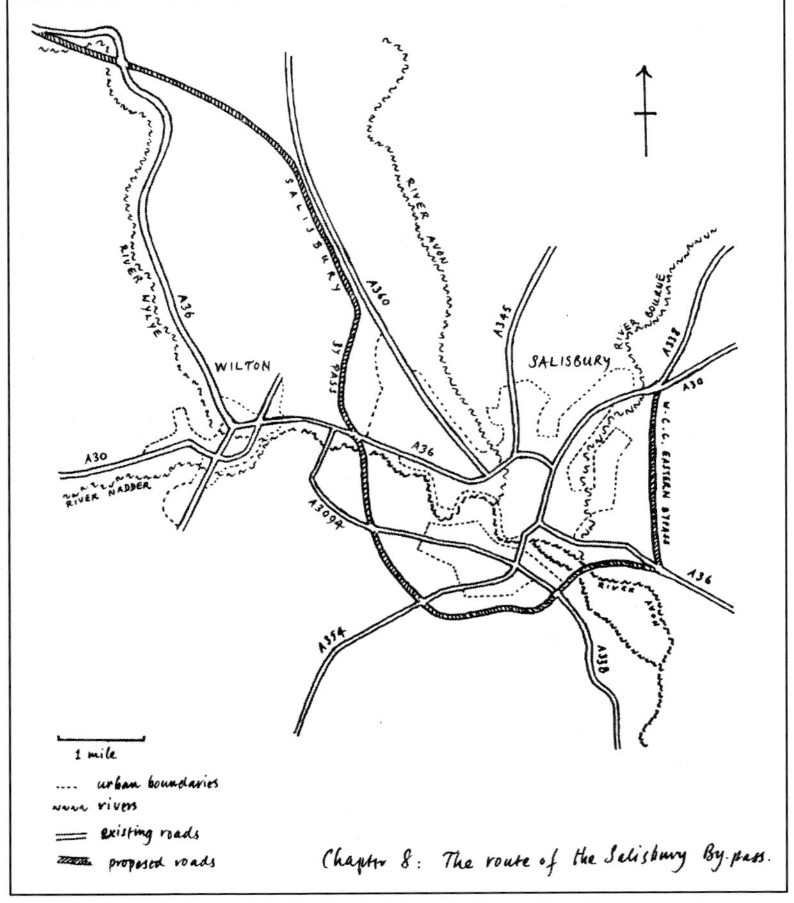

By-pass route sketch map. Although laid before the public in a year long enquiry from 1993, the plans echo those published in the 1965 Town Centre plan, and to a degree those in Sharp's 1949 proposals.

Sharp's view of Newer Sarum. A new road is driven through St Thomas's Square – thus restoring an ancient through route – but the whole of the quarter from Woolley and Wallis's Castle Auction Mart through to the Shoulder of Mutton and the parade of shops on the north side of Bridge Street would have disappeared. At the top right, where Salisbury Library is now, there would have been a new civic hall; the Bishop's Mill would have been the museum, and one of the flanking wings would have been a new library. The Maltings, beyond, would have remained.

stimulated consideration by local authorities and academics of how communities work. The built environment was seen anew as the framework within which communities functioned. Transport – particularly in the age of mass private motoring, when its manifestations are the result of an aggregate of individual choices – has for 50 years been identified as one of the great challenges for the planners.

In 1949 Thomas Sharp was commissioned by the City Council to address the major concerns then felt to be facing the city: the quality of its housing and its infrastructure, including the road system. If, and as, more people chose to use cars to visit the city, for business or pleasure, and if Salisbury retained its pivotal position in the transport network that it had held since time immemorial, what were the implications for the city's network of streets, and what might the solutions be? Sharp's vision satisfied – or at least addressed – two criteria. His plan sought to ease congestion by broadening a number of streets to create an inner ring-road, and to provide access to new facilities within the city, routing new roads so as to lead to and offer views of the city's mediaeval heritage. However, in the process, a dual carriageway would have run from Fisherton Street, behind the Maltings to Castle Street, and cut through the four northernmost Chequers, before turning south along the line of St Edmund's Church Street as far as Gigant Street. There would have been five roundabouts, and a sixth in the Market Place. He also envisaged a southern bypass with a feeder road along Britford Lane.

Sharp's plan was not adopted; instead, a two-stage relief scheme was planned, broadly addressing Sharp's objectives. The first stage, an inner ring-road, would address the needs of commuters, shoppers and visitors by directing traffic around the outskirts of the historic city centre and into parking sited at the periphery and in the less historically-significant areas of the city centre. This first stage would also serve the needs of through traffic until an outer ring-road could be built. Plans considered in the mid to late 1960s by both city and county planners show both stages. The outer ring-road thus prefigured by two decades the scheme proposed in the 1980s when the A36 Southampton–Bristol route was designated as part of the national road network along with the M27 South Coast motorway and the A34.

Sharp's view of Newer Sarum. Another new road from a roundabout swings behind the Infirmary to join New Street, giving a 'new direct view … for dramatic effect.'

The inner ring-road, Churchill Way, was built between 1962 and 1969: it had two fewer roundabouts than Sharp's scheme and was achieved mainly at the expense of 19th-century housing. Major sacrifices included the overshadowing of the Green Croft and the demolition of Moorland House. Unbelievably, Sharp's ideas still enjoyed some currency as late as 1965, his road through the northern Chequers featuring in the WCC Town Centre Plan of that year.

When, in 1988, the second stage was mooted, opinion was sought on three possible routes, two to the south and one to the east and north. All three routes would have provided relief for villages in the Wylye Valley, eliminating a notorious accident black spot south of Stapleford. The favoured route lay to the south – as it had done since Sharp's plan 40 years previously – but between the initial consultation and the publication of the proposals an astonishing sleight of hand occurred, as the scheme now laid before the public comprised, instead of a single carriageway, a dual carriageway with eight junctions. It would be 11 miles long and cost £76 million. A year-long public inquiry, the forum for vigorous debate, followed from 1993 to April 1994. Arguments against ranged from the fantastic – that the road would traverse the water-meadows from which Constable painted the cathedral – to the soberly accurate – that only about 5 per cent of the traffic overloading the existing road was through traffic.

Nevertheless, approval was given, but, perhaps in the light of the furore engendered by the nearby Winchester and Newbury by-passes, the Government referred the matter to the Highways Agency for further consideration. The matter remained undecided until the election of May 1997, when the incoming administration cancelled the project. Where that decision has left Salisbury is considered in our final chapter.

Chapter 9

Ground bass: 'The sick and needy shall not always be forgotten'

Mediaeval Hospitals

IF IT is the mark of a civilised society that it cares for its vulnerable members, then Salisbury can lay claim to civilisation from its earliest days and before. The first sign of this sense of a duty of care was St Nicholas's Hospital, founded sometime in the first quarter of the 13th century. But the hospital's function can only be gauged with any degree of certainty from 14 October 1245, when it was refounded by Bishop Bingham. He charged its warden and brethren with the care of the weak and the sick and the maintenance of the bridge, as well as the religious duties associated with the Chapel of St John, on the bridge, and with the parish of St Nicholas, which was extinguished only when St Edmund's came into being in 1269. There are scattered references to the hospital's role in caring for the sick up to the time when Bishop Beauchamp granted new statutes in 1478, which cast its role much more as an almshouse, for both sexes, including married couples. Admission of the latter could prove problematic: in 1605, one couple, 'Newton and his wyfe' had a quarrel at dinner and ended up throwing bones around, and in 1626 the hospital's patron, the Earl of Pembroke, forbade the Master from admitting any more married couples as some had hitherto 'proved both burthensome and troublesome to the house'. The hospital survived the Reformation, despite attempts to dissolve it as a chantry chapel, and the Civil War, and continues today to provide for six men and six women.

The other mediaeval foundation which survives to this day is Trinity Hospital, founded in around 1370 by Agnes, wife of John Bottenham, who, according to legend, was an innkeeper and whorehouse madame, and the hospital was built on the site of the brothel in expiation of the founder's past life. It was refounded by John Chandler in 1396, with the stated objectives of receiving and caring for the infirm and the poor. Care was given to 12 permanent residents, male or female, and also to 18 visitors who were offered three days' stay, or until restored in health. As with any such institution in the Middle Ages, organised religious observance and private prayer was prescribed for the residents, and as

St Nicholas' Hospital. A woodcut from Hall's *Picturesque memorials*, 1834. The institution is contemporary with the earliest years of the new city, but its life as an almshouse can be dated only from 1478.

St Nicholas' Hospital, Harnham, 2002.

Trinity Hospital. Like all but one of the other almshouses in Salisbury, Trinity Hospital is part of the life of the city rather than the Close; like most others the individual dwellings face onto a courtyard at right angles to the street, as did many other dwellings between the 16th and early 20th centuries. At the end of the courtyard is the simple chapel.

this included prayers for the hospital's benefactors Trinity Hospital must have had the character of a chantry, though the range of its activities as listed in 1400 was impressive: 'the hungry were fed, the thirsty had drink, the naked were clothed, the sick were comforted, the dead were buried, the mad were restored to their reason, orphans and widows were nourished and lying-in women were kept till they were delivered, recovered and churched'. Perhaps for these reasons and the fact that the mayor appointed the master, the hospital avoided closure during the Reformation and survives still, providing for 10 deserving individuals.

Almshouses

After the Reformation, a steady stream of benefactions and bequests resulted in the foundation of almshouses, of which only two, Sutton's and Brown's, have failed to survive. The earliest, Brickett's, was founded in 1534, to house 'five poor men or women, for Christ's sake, to pray for me', and thus still retained a link between the founder's care for the living, and his beneficiaries' care for his immortal soul. Eyre's Hospital, originally dating from 1617, and Margaret Blechynden's almshouses, built in 1683, were founded by members of the Eyre family, while Taylor's Almshouses, of 1698, and Frowd's Hospital, 1750, are close neighbours, both facing St Edmund's Church. While many almshouses were endowed from bequests, two from the end of the 18th century, Hussey's, in Castle Street, founded 1794, and Sarah Hayter's, in Fisherton Anger, were established during their founders' lifetimes, Hussey's to mark 20 years of his service to the city in Parliament. All of these houses were for between half-a-dozen and 20 beneficiaries; their 20th-century equivalents, from Brympton House at Harnham to Steve Biddle House, provide a home for nearly 150 more. Steve Biddle House, offering sheltered housing with additional support – a midday meal and enhanced social facilities – is an innovative approach to the need to provide care in the community as defined in the 1993 Act.

Frowd's Almshouses. At his death in 1720, Edward Frowd was said to be 'a Great Benefactor to his parish', and his intention had been to provide for 24 people, but his will was contested, and not finally proved for another half-century. Facing St Edmund's Church, Frowd's Hospital, founded in 1750, provided for six men and six women.

Hussey's Almshouses. William Hussey had a distinguished career in public life and was an MP for the city at the time of his gift, which was built in the site of the Castle Gate and provided for 10 elderly and frail married couples; subsequent redesign of the accommodation now provides for up to 24 people.

The Infirmary

While the pre-Reformation hospitals gave shelter to the needy and care to the sick – and the words hospital, hospice, hostel and hotel all come from a common Latin root – the second function generally arose from the duty of caring for travellers or strangers, people who by virtue of their journeying were cut off from the care they would receive at home. St Nicholas, dedicatee of Salisbury's earliest hospital, was the patron saint of travellers. Otherwise care for the sick was limited to occupants already in the hospitals as deserving cases. The concept of the hospital as an infirmary, provided as a public service, is a relatively modern idea. With the Reformation some of the great London hospitals survived, such as the Bethlehem, Christ's, St Bartholomew's and St Thomas', and medicine became a secular profession. We have seen that locally, in response to the plague, sufferers might be placed in a pest-house primarily to isolate them from all except their carers, and recovery depended on rest and the body's own recuperative powers.

By the 18th century, the notion that surgery and medicine might be two sides of the same coin began to gain currency, as a result partly of the discoveries of the scientific revolution, like the circulation of the blood and the efficacy of inoculation, and partly of the work of pioneers like Dr Turberville. Hitherto, surgery had been a branch of the trade of the barber-surgeons, while physicians had been prevented by the Hippocratic oath from taking the knife to any of their patients. Smallpox was endemic in Salisbury from around 1700, and there were epidemics in 1723 and 1752, and it was against that background, and a growing sense that disease and infirmity were open to challenge, that prompted the founding of the Infirmary. Others had already been established in York, Exeter, Bristol and Winchester.

The terms of Lord Feversham of Downton's will in 1763 prompted speedy action, and in consequence of a resolution of the Corporation in March 1766, meetings were held in August and September of that year to open a fund-raising subscription list and to constitute a governing body for the hospital. By October, some cottages between the Fisherton Bridge and the Bull Inn had been bought, and Mrs S. Causeway, assistant matron at the Royal Hampshire County Hospital, had been appointed matron. In April 1767 Mrs Causeway

The Infirmary Building, 2002. The conversion of the Infirmary into private apartments has restored the original battlemented parapet: the two wings were added during the 19th century.

The Infirmary as originally envisaged, 1766. The appeal for funds was accompanied by this engraving, which shows the Infirmary substantially as it was built.

appointed two nurses, and at the end of the month the hospital admitted its first patients. The establishment, apart from the committee of officers who managed the hospital's affairs, comprised two surgeons and two physicians, who gave their services voluntarily, two apothecaries, the matron, two nurses, a porter, a messenger and a chaplain. The chaplain's annual salary was £30, Mrs Causeway's £16, the nurses' and the porter's £6 and the messenger's £5. The porter's salary was well-earned: he brewed, he baked bread, he ground the medicines, he gardened, he was the handyman and he kept watch at the gate, not least to ensure the inmates didn't escape. Of the Infirmary in its earliest days the ***Salisbury Guide*** of 1769 wrote 'There is no friend to humanity but ought to encourage this extensive charity; the pleasing reflection of having it in one's power, at a small expence, of having numbers of poor, indigent persons cured, must be very great to a good mind: parishes particularly ought to subscribe, as thereby their sick poor will be more speedily and more effectually be healed, than they possibly can at home.'

However, there were limitations on who might be admitted, and when. One had to be recommended by a benefactor or subscriber to be admitted; and 'No woman big with child, no child under 7 years old, except in extraordinary cases ...; none disordered in their senses, suspected to have the small-pox, itch, ulcers in the legs, cancers, consumptions, dropsies, epilepsies, are received as in-patients.' Patients were admitted and discharged on Saturdays between 11am and 1pm. The Infirmary treated many as out-patients, and if they lived more than seven miles away they were given 1s a week to help defray their accommodation expenses (typically around 3s 6d weekly), but begging was prohibited on pain of discharge. Despite these constraints, the Infirmary admitted 798 in-patients and 1,706 out-patients while the new building was under construction. Costing just under £9,000, the building was declared open on 17 August 1771.

Space was constantly at a premium, admissions rising by almost 50 per cent in seven years. With patients having to share beds, and with outbreaks of disease and infestation of rats, accommodation had to be reorganised and, eventually, augmented. The east wing was built in 1845, and in 1869 the west wing, together with improvements in the east wing on the advice of Florence Nightingale. Treatments were simple – herbal remedies, cupping, purging, bloodletting with leeches. Operations were rarely undertaken and then only after a conference of all the surgical and medical staff. Until the advent of anaesthetics, speed was of the essence, with amputations and bladder stone removals done in a matter of minutes: but until the advent of antiseptics, wound infection and even gangrene frequently occurred, with fatal consequences. Yet many were given back their lives, and many more were cured simply by being cared for, and, in W.H. Hudson's words, throughout the county 'the "Infirmary" is a name of the deepest meaning, and a place of many sad and tender and beautiful associations'.

By the 1870s some 90 operations were undertaken annually, by the 1920s and 1930s almost 1,000, and by the 1960s nearly 10,000. By 1919 ever-growing demands prompted the Infirmary's management to consider refurbishing the building, rebuilding on the existing site, or building a new hospital elsewhere. Moves toward the last step were undertaken with the purchase of Butts Farm in 1921, but when the costings were completed, the first option was found to be the most cost effective. Not until 1993 was the Salisbury District General Hospital opened at Odstock, where since World War Two there had been a military hospital, later taken over by the County Council and maintained as a specialist unit for the treatment of burns. The Infirmary remains, now converted into apartments.

Laverstock House and Fisherton House: the Care of the Mentally Ill

In one area of medicine Salisbury was a centre of national importance from early days: its provision for the mentally ill was the largest concentration outside London. The first mental hospital, or madhouse as it was known in the 18th century, was in Laverstock, established about 15 years before William Finch's arrival in 1779. His advertisement in the ***Salisbury Journal*** of 8 February 1779 promised that 'The friends of such unfortunate persons who are committed to his care, may depend on their being treated with the greatest tenderness and humanity, by their faithful humble servant William Finch'. He was the first of four generations of Finches to be associated with psychiatric hospitals from the 18th to the 20th centuries. By the early 1800s, Laverstock House had over 100 patients, and William Finch the younger acquired the manor house at Fisherton and opened it in 1813 as a new asylum.

CURE of LUNATICS.
WILLIAM FINCH, of MILFORD, near Saliſbury, having for many years had great ſucceſs in curing people diſordered in their ſenſes, takes the liberty to acquaint the pubic, that he ſtill continues to take charge of unhappy perſons of both ſexes in every ſtage of that malady. The many cures he has performed on Lunatics ſent from different parts of the kingdom, particularly from the counties of Dorſet, Hants, and Wilts, can be atteſted by Gentlemen of great credit and veracity. It is with the greateſt ſatisfaction he can ſay, that every perſon he has had charge of, has, with the bleſſing of God, been cured and diſcharged from his houſe perfectly well. The friends of ſuch unfortunate perſons who are committed to his care, may depend on their being treated with the greateſt tenderneſs and humanity, by their faithful humble ſervant, WILLIAM FINCH, Milford.

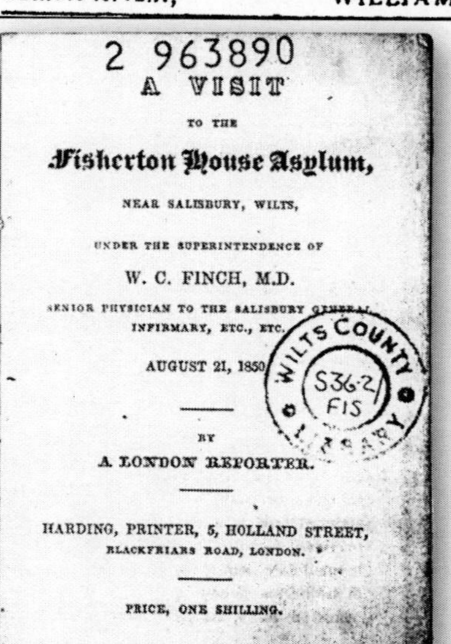

A VISIT
TO THE
Fisherton House Asylum,
NEAR SALISBURY, WILTS,
UNDER THE SUPERINTENDENCE OF
W. C. FINCH, M.D.
SENIOR PHYSICIAN TO THE SALISBURY GENERAL INFIRMARY, ETC., ETC.
AUGUST 21, 1850.
BY
A LONDON REPORTER.
HARDING, PRINTER, 5, HOLLAND STREET,
BLACKFRIARS ROAD, LONDON.
PRICE, ONE SHILLING.

(Above) First *Salisbury Journal* advertisement announcing William Finch's services in the care of the mentally ill, 8 February 1779. (Left) Title-page of 1850 report on life in Fisherton House.

By then the care of the mentally ill was regarded as a medical specialism: the second William was qualified, and ran two madhouses in London, in Kensington and Chelsea, in addition to his Wiltshire enterprises. Fisherton outgrew Laverstock within a few decades: by 1854 it was licensed for 214 patients, and was thus the largest institution of its kind outside London, and by 1878 it was licensed for 672 patients. Apart from fee-paid clients, Laverstock and Fisherton also cared for paupers who were too disruptive for the workhouses, but in 1851 a county asylum was opened for the deranged poor, and Laverstock, in common with most other private madhouses, concentrated on private patients. In 1854 William Corbin Finch disposed of Laverstock, while at Fisherton care had branched out to include that of criminal lunatics, a specialism it retained until 1872, when the care of such patients was transferred entirely to Broadmoor, opened eight years earlier. But Fisherton continued to care for paupers, receiving them from as far afield as Portsmouth and London.

As we have seen from Finch's advertisement, the work of the asylums and life therein was premised on the awareness that their charges were afflicted and their treatment was grounded in compassion. In a handbill published by his son in December 1807, Laverstock was said to be 'on a healthy eminence with many acres of gardens and pleasure grounds for the exercise and amusement of the patients', while in 1850 in a one-shilling booklet 'a London Reporter' visiting Fisherton wrote of its being 'happily situated to receive the uninterrupted pure and genial air of an open country', and referred to 'huge trays of varied provisions of the best character'. In the Female Department, 'usefulness, reading, needlework [and] embroidery' attest to occupational therapy known to have been offered at Fisherton since 1829, while one patient named Card, who wrote music and played the violin, offered the testimonial that he was 'never so happy in my life'. Occasionally, there was a darker side to life at Fisherton: the Lunacy Commissioners reported adversely in 1850, 1865 and 1883, while some of the treatments, ranging from a 'rotatory chair' in 1815 to the admittedly rare use of the straitjacket, even as late as 1937, appear instances of cruelty for kindness' sake. But the objectives were cure or rehabilitation: Dr Finch claimed that of the 42 patients admitted in 1814–15, 22 had been cured, while in 1847 his son identified four states of mental illness as mania, melancholia, epilepsy and paralysis, with detailed treatments for all. As in other branches of medicine, enormous advances have been made, and today, newly restored to very much its original appearance, the Old Manor remains to meet its founders' objectives.

Higher Education

From its earliest years, education was integral to the life of the new city of Salisbury. The earliest concentration of scholars was to be found among the canons whom Richard Poore had appointed to his chapter, and the chancellor directed a school of theology. The Franciscan friars had established themselves across the street from the close between 1225 and 1228 on land lent to them by Bishop Poore, and from 1238, students from Oxford had resorted to Salisbury in times of plague and other difficulties. It is likely that one such exodus prompted Bishop Bridport to found De Vaux College for 'poor, needy, well-born and teachable scholars', in 1261, predating Merton College's foundation by two years and thereby being the first university college in England. Its main objective was the study of theology prior to ordination at Salisbury and a living within the diocese, though its students occasionally studied law and medicine. It was perhaps because its main objective was to secure parish clergy, rather than to be a freestanding educational institution that De Vaux College never aspired to become England's third university. Salisbury's mediaeval scholarly community

The King's House, from Hall's ***Picturesque memorials***, 1834. So named because during the occupancy of Sir Thomas Sadler, diocesan registrar, King James I stayed here in 1610 and 1613. The house has had a long and chequered career, ranging from prebendal mansion for the Abbots of Sherborne, to a private dwelling, to a women's teacher training college from 1841 to 1978, when it became the home for the Salisbury and South Wiltshire Museum.

De Vaux College from Hall's ***Picturesque memorials***, 1834. By the time of this engraving, the college had been all but demolished and replaced by a terrace of houses: a small fragment of the masonry has been incorporated into the new building.

was completed with the transfer by 1281 of the Dominican community from Wilton to Fisherton Anger, on a site across the road from the later gaol and Infirmary.

With the college's closure at the Reformation, tertiary education was not to return to Salisbury until 1841, when the Diocesan Training College was founded, followed by the Theological College in 1860. The training college, later named the College of Sarum St Michael, provided teacher training for women, initially for the diocese, and later nationally. It was a victim of the move in the mid-1970s towards diversification and expansion in public-sector higher education, and closed in 1978. Its premises have a new life as the Salisbury and South Wiltshire Museum, the Wiltshire County Council Conservation Laboratory and as private apartments. Similarly, the theological college came to be amalgamated with the Wells Theological College, and, with the transfer of teaching to Wells in 1994, now remains as Sarum College, a conference and education centre. Today the provision of higher education remains with the external courses of study available at Salisbury College, while plans for a University of Swindon and Wiltshire are currently in abeyance.

Schools – Up to the 19th Century

The education of the young can be traced to Salisbury's earliest days, before the move from Old Sarum, for John of Salisbury is known to have been educated there before 1091. Teaching of the choristers was divided

The City Grammar School, founded in 1569, perhaps as an assertion of power by the civic authorities, moved into these premises in castle street in 1624, almost opposite Chipper Lane. Throughout its history the City Grammar School appears to have been pretty ineffectual, and by the time it was wound up, its pupils were receiving their education from another teacher in the city, Mr Bridger.

The Close Grammar School provided general schooling, as distinct from voice training, for the choristers, but it was also to be maintained 'like a free school and common Grammar School'. The school evolved into the Cathedral School, and moved into the Bishop's Palace in 1947. By 1980 the old school house, known as Wren Hall, was taken over for cathedral administration.

The Bishop's Palace, as depicted in Hall's ***Picturesque memorials***, 1834. Even though its use has changed dramatically – for it is now the Cathedral School – it is readily recognisable from this engraving.

between the Choristers' School and the Grammar School. The latter, which stood outside the Close, near St Ann's Gate, provided for pupils within the city as well as the cathedral's choristers and its altarists who maintained the altars and assisted with services, perhaps in preparation for the priesthood. There were times when the Grammar School apparently ceased to function, for there are, for instance, no records of it after 1470. In addition, teaching would have been provided by the parish clergy, the friars and others. The Reformation brought about gains and losses, in education as in other aspects of life. The friaries were dissolved, and with them went their teaching. But the Grammar School was revived in 1540, and re-established in the Close. At that point it became more or less exclusively a school for the Close, and specifically the choristers, eventually becoming the Cathedral School. The corporation responded by appealing to the King that he found a school in Salisbury, arguing that 'the Cytye of Newe Sarum is a goodly Cytye and well peopled, as is well-known, full of youth'. The appeal was accompanied by the frankly disingenuous suggestion that chantry revenues with which the grammar schools at Trowbridge and Bradford had been endowed should be diverted to Salisbury.

The City Grammar School was founded in 1569, and run from a room in the George Inn, whence it transferred to premises in Castle Street in 1624, on account of 'the inconveniency of coming to the schollers by the Taphouse and inne'. It was open to pupils from all stations, with the quarterly fee of 7s 6d being remitted in cases of poverty. Throughout its history the City Grammar School appears to have been pretty ineffectual: from 1743 its master was also paid £20 per annum from the Eyre Foundation to teach at the school attached to St Thomas's, and the office of the school's last master, the Revd Hodgson, from 1804 to 1864, was the final straw. He never had more than 22 pupils, and his roll declined to seven in 1855, and three by the time of his resignation. By then most of his pupils had transferred to Mr Bridger's school. Apart from the Grammar School, education was provided by private schools, of which there are references to five by 1714, or by charities, the latter from the early 18th century onwards. A survey of charity schools in 1731 refers to three such schools in Salisbury, providing for 200 pupils. A further three were founded during the course of the 18th century, and of these, the Godolphin School, established in 1784, continues to this day. The curriculum in the 18th century included dancing, reading, writing, casting accounts and 'the business of Housewifry', and the teaching in the Victorian era involved endless rote learning.

In the late 1850s, the Revd William Warburton, one of Her Majesty's Inspectors, was appointed to survey all the schools in Wiltshire 'for the children of the labouring classes': his report was published in February 1859, and by then in Salisbury there were numerous private academies. But much more significant were the foundations of a nationwide system of education which were the object of Warburton's survey. In it he describes, apart from the model school attached to the Diocesan Training School (80 pupils) and the Union

Henry Hatcher. Hatcher's lasting fame rests on his contribution to Colt Hoare's history of southern Wiltshire – the first comprehensive history of Salisbury, written between 1836 and 1843. After his career as the city's postmaster from 1817 was cut short in 1822, Hatcher became master of one of the city's many private schools in the early 19th century in Endless Street. He described teaching as the 'best point of profit that I have yet exercised, and I prefer solid pudding to empty praise.'

(i.e. Workhouse) School (20–30), local schools under the aegis of the Church of England and the Nonconformist churches, providing for between 750 and 800 pupils. In addition there were nine dame schools (120 pupils), and sundry private schools (170 pupils). Warburton's comments range from 'certificated master of much ability .... This school is one of the best with which I am acquainted' (St Martin's Boys' School) to 'a mistress of the old school, who thoroughly understands her own system, and contemns new lights' (Gigant Street Infants' School). Scarcely a decade later, in 1870, Forster's Education Act was passed, which raised the school leaving age to 13, and established school boards with the power to set up schools without any religious affiliation. In Salisbury this sparked a tremendous controversy, and led to the educational provision in Salisbury today, which differs from that throughout the rest of Wiltshire in retaining selection.

Schools – into the 20th Century

The Nonconformists in Salisbury welcomed the prospect of a non-denominational school on the rates, and closed two of their schools to expedite the process. However, the School Board in Salisbury was dominated by Anglicans, who were prepared to expand the existing national (Anglican) schools, but not build a board school. It went so far as to found a Salisbury Church Day School Association to counter the Nonconformists' campaign, and its obduracy was a matter for debate in the House of Commons in 1890. The result, at considerable expense to the diocese, was the foundation of a boys' secondary school (a personal ambition of the bishop, John Wordsworth) which later became Bishop Wordsworth's School, and three other new church schools. Not until 1924 did Salisbury gain its first non-denominational school, built by the City Council (by then the Local Education Authority) in Highbury Avenue to serve the needs of the new council estate. Secondary education was extended with the opening of the South Wilts Grammar School for Girls in 1927 and the conversion of St Edmund's and St Thomas's schools into, respectively, girls' and boys' secondary schools in 1928. Since then St Edmund's has moved out to Laverstock, to be joined by Highbury School, now renamed Wyvern College and designated a technology college. Also in Laverstock, St Joseph's RC Secondary Modern School was founded in 1964. St Thomas's, meanwhile, opened on a new site on Bemerton Heath in 1957, where on an adjoining site the Westwood County Girls' Secondary Modern School was opened in 1958. In 1973 the two schools combined to become Westwood St Thomas's, distinctive in Salisbury for several reasons. Like St Joseph's it is co-educational, and like Wyvern College it is a technology college. But it has the additional claims upon our attention of being the city's only comprehensive school, and of having the city's largest sixth form, and of being the third stage in the system of the first and middle schools. Despite its educational and social benefits and the loyal support of the communities it serves in South Wiltshire, it seems likely this system will soon be abolished.

Meanwhile, throughout the 19th and 20th centuries, private education flourished. The Cleveland House School was opened in Kelsey Road in 1880, and prepared pupils for the College of Preceptors,

Cambridge and London University matriculation and Civil Service entrance exams; Uplands, a large bungalow on the corner of Dorset and Cambridge Roads, was built as a school for 120 pupils aged 4–11. *Kelly's Directory* for 1964 lists 15 schools, catering for all age groups.

Further Education

The need for further education in Salisbury was first addressed by the Mechanics' Institution from February 1833 until its demise in 1840. There were other initiatives, such as St Elizabeth's School and House of Industry. The provision scattered throughout the city came together into two colleges. Salisbury College of Art could trace its origins back to 1871 with the building of new premises for the Literary and Scientific Institution, and the establishment soon after of a School of Art. The Salisbury and South Wilts College of

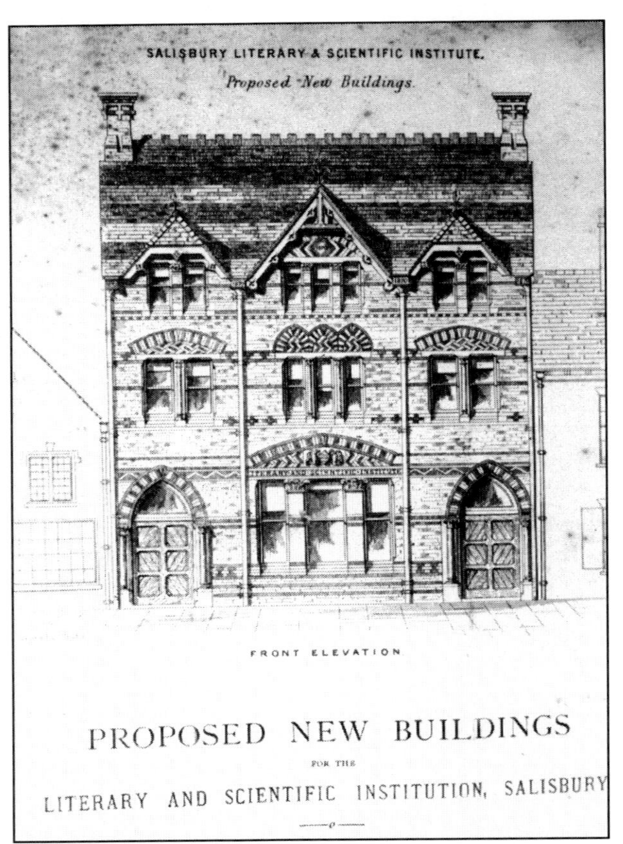

The Literary and Scientific Institution (the Hamilton Hall), New Street. This illustration, from the prospectus, shows the building which replaced the city's first purpose-built theatre. It is recognisable today, although now commercial office premises.

Further Education was split between the Castle Road (Engineering, Building and Science Department) and Churchfields (offices, Commercial and Domestic Science Departments). In the 1960s the two colleges came together on the Southampton Road campus, and in 1993 they joined to become Salisbury College.

Crime and Punishment

By an odd irony, the Infirmary, one of the city's most potent symbols of its care for its people, stands on the site of an equally powerful sign of its need to punish its miscreants. For, directly to the left of the cluster of cottages which became the Infirmary, stood the city's prison, and when the new County Gaol was built at the bottom of Devizes Road between 1818 and 1822, the old prison was acquired by the Infirmary at a cost of £1,750; when the Infirmary's east wing was built in 1845, one small corner was left standing, bearing, as it does to this day, a reminder of its earlier role. Opposite the Infirmary is a yet more poignant reminder of an earlier age's idea of what was beyond the pale. What is now a public house was once a memorial to three Protestants. John Maundrel, John Spicer and William Coberley were burnt at the stake at Fisherton on 24 March 1556 having been found guilty of heresy following their disruption of the Sunday service at their home village of Keevil. Executions, such as those of the Duke of Buckingham in 1483 for treason, and of Charles, Lord Stourton, for murder in 1557, were public spectacles, as were the consequences, such as the portion of Jack Cade displayed in Salisbury following a citizen's part in the murder of Bishop Ayscough.

We have already seen above how heavy the penalties could be for both crimes such as witchcraft and activities in support of Captain Swing. What is perhaps not so commonly realised is the variety of crimes attracting harsh penalties a mere six generations ago. Thus, passing forged banknotes (in 1802, 1805, 1816 and 1820) and theft of livestock (thrice in 1804, twice in 1803 and 1806, and once each in 1807, 1815, 1817 and 1828), both attracted the death penalty, while lesser charges, such as 'the cropping and spoiling of timber trees', incurred penalties ranging from a public whipping to transportation. One of the most gruesome aspects of the due process of law was the extent to which

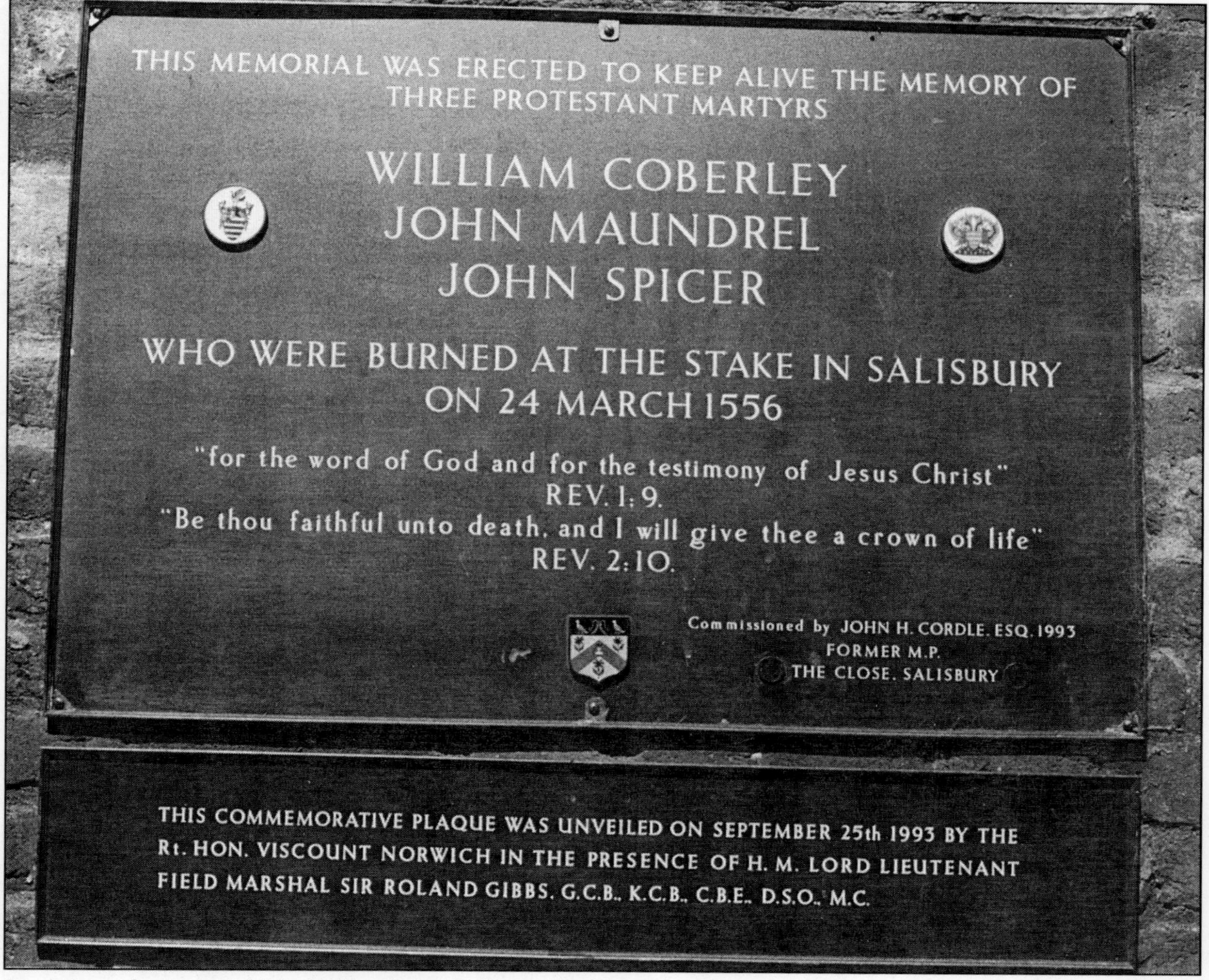

Inscription to the memory of Coberley, Maundrel and Spicer, just inside St Ann's Gate.

it was made a public spectacle. Until the early 19th century murderers were hanged where their crime was committed, and one, Robert Watkins, tried and condemned at the assizes of 1819 for the murder of Stephen Rodney, was taken to the scene of his crime, Moor Stones, near Purton, together with his coffin, to be dispatched in view of some 15,000 onlookers.

Gradually, however, attitudes changed. Only a handful of people were present at the last public execution in Salisbury, in 1855, when William Wright was hanged for the murder of Ann Collins at Lydiard Tregoze. The pillory was abolished in 1837, but the stocks remained in place for another 20 years. Their presence evoked the young Dickens's tears, but only because his parents refused him the money for missiles to pelt the convicted. In 1858 they were used for the last time, to punish John Selloway for drunkenness, on his refusal to pay a 5s fine.

Chapter 10

Grace Notes: Salisbury at Leisure

Pageants and carnivals

IF ONE mark of a civilised society is that it cares for its weaker members, another, surely, is that it knows how to enjoy itself. We have noted the importance of pageantry in the Middle Ages, and, in one form or another, and with different motivations,

(Above and top right) Views from either end of Queen Street.

The Peace Festival at Salisbury, 19 May 1856. The lithograph made by Walter Tiffin and published by Brown shows the Giant, Hob-Nob and morris dancers as well as ranks of tables for the open-air dinner in the Market Place, at which 3,000 were seated. They dined on 8,000lb of roast meat and 4,000lb of plum pudding, washed down with 900 gallons of beer.

The Peace Festival of 1856. One of the earliest photographs records the view towards the Castle Road corner of the Market Place, and, predating the Market House, rather more of No.1 Castle Street than survives today. The last such 'sit-down meal' was held for the coronation of George V in 1911.

(Below) The Druid Procession, 27 June 1832. Within a few years of the emergence of modern Druidism in the early 19th century, the movement had a role in society not dissimilar from that of the Freemasons and the friendly societies. On the second of Salisbury's three days of celebration on the passage of the Reform Bill, the Druids headed the grand procession through the city which preceded the public dinner in the Market Place. The events were recorded in the ***Salisbury Journal*** and the August issue of the ***Druids' Magazine***, and the scene was preserved in this engraving in which the view of the buildings along one side of the Market Place (Queen Street) is a valuable historical record.

The Coronation Pageant of 1902. The Female Lodge of the Independent Order of Foresters portrays the Nations of the World.

The Celebration of Salisbury's Seventh Centenary, 1927. The Giant, processing down Castle Street, leads the parade for Salisbury's fifth century.

Every year the parishoners of Great Wishford travel to the cathedral on Oak Apple Day, 29 May, to reassert their ancient right to gather wood from Grovely Wood. This picture is of the 1998 procession.

Morris men in the Market Place, July 2002. A carnival atmosphere often pervades the city centre in summer, when concerts, morris-dancing displays and other events take place.

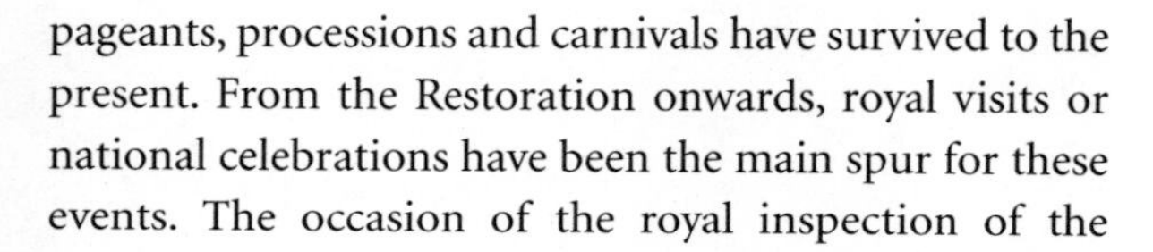

pageants, processions and carnivals have survived to the present. From the Restoration onwards, royal visits or national celebrations have been the main spur for these events. The occasion of the royal inspection of the cathedral, newly restored, in 1792, was a cause for public celebration, and the Peace of Amiens in 1802 and that of Paris in 1814 were marked by processions and fireworks. The latter event was marked, as before and

The October Fair in the late 1920s. First established in 1270, the October Fair has for many decades been a funfair.

The keyless Dean organ 'The Happy Wanderer', fundraising for the Mayor's charity, October Fair, late 1990s.

'Side Winder' ride, late 1990s at the October Fair.

since, by a great feast in the Market Place. In 1814, two sheep and an ox were roasted whole, and 2,500 loaves and 12 hogsheads of beer were consumed. In the last century, there were pageants to mark the peace in 1919, the 700th anniversary of the founding of the city in 1927, at the coronations and the jubilees, while the St George's Day celebrations have been revived in recent years.

Music

We have seen also the importance of music in the life of the city, and music festivals were held annually from 1742 to 1789, again from 1792 to 1796, in 1800 and then every three years from 1804 to 1828. The rich musical life of the city continued in various guises throughout

The Salisbury Philharmonic Society, founded in 1894. A group portrait, featuring its founder and conductor, Alfred Foley, who was a music dealer in New Canal.

the 19th century, with William Price Aylward, piano and music seller and teacher, organising subscription concerts in the Assembly Rooms, where Franz Liszt gave a recital in 1840. The Sarum Choral Society, founded in 1848, and itself the reincarnation of the Salisbury Musical Society in existence in 1801, was refounded by Sir Walter Alcock, the cathedral organist, from 1916 to 1947, under the earlier name in 1923. It gives two concerts each year, of major set-pieces like Britten's ***War Requiem*** or Walton's ***Belshazzar's Feast.*** The Salisbury Orchestral Society, also founded by Alcock, continues the tradition of the Salisbury Philharmonic Society, founded and conducted by Alfred Foley. Other groups include the Sarum Chamber Orchestra, the Salisbury Operatic Society, founded in 1908, and the Farrant Singers, founded in 1958. Even under wartime constraints, the city enjoyed rich opportunities: in June 1942 and August 1943, at the city's larger cinemas, the London Philharmonic Orchestra playing 'at pre-war strength – 70 players' gave concerts which included Beethoven's ***Pastoral Symphony***, Tchaikovsky's ***Fourth Symphony*** and Richard Strauss's symphonic poem ***Don Juan.*** Sacred music has its own festival, the Southern Cathedrals Festival, which was held from 1904 to 1932, and inaugurated again in 1960: it rotates between Salisbury, Winchester and Chichester. The cathedral serves the city as a concert venue for medium and large-scale orchestral works, while the Mediaeval Hall in the Close is the setting for chamber music.

The Primitive Methodist Chapel in Fisherton Street, which Albany Ward acquired from the trustees on the undertaking it was to become a garage. Ironically, his Palace Theatre in Endless Street did end up as a garage.

Theatre and Film

Live drama in Salisbury suffered mixed fortunes after the New Theatre in New Street was demolished to make way for the Hamilton Hall, which housed the Literary and Scientific Institution and the School of Art. The Hamilton Hall was also a venue for theatre, as were the Assembly Rooms; then in September 1889 the County Hall with 1,000 seats was opened, on the corner of Endless Street and Chipper Lane. In 1908 the Bristol entrepreneur Albany Ward first showed motion pictures there, and between 1910 and 1916 he leased the County Hall, renaming it the Palace, and opened two new auditoriums, the New Theatre in Castle Street and the Picture House in Fisherton Street. The New Theatre and the Palace showed both cinema and live theatre. But with the arrival of the talkies, and of major players like the Rank Organisation, Ward decided it was time to quit, and neither the Palace nor the New Theatre survived Ward's departure in 1931 by many years, while the

Spoof Weimar Republic 100,000-mark note to advertise the three-act farce ***Tons of Money***, transferred from the Aldwych to the Palace Theatre, Salisbury, in September 1924.

Picture House was taken over by the Rank Organisation. By 1937, Salisbury had three new cinemas, in the form of the Regal in Endless Street, opposite the Palace, the Gaumont in New Canal which had John Hall's house as its foyer and the New Picture House in Fisherton Street, near to the old Picture House.

The old Picture House was put up for sale, but there were no takers, and with the war the building was requisitioned as a drill hall. Then ENSA took the building over and opened it in October 1943 as the Garrison Theatre, a services establishment. At the end of the war, with the impending departure of ENSA, the Salisbury and District Society of Arts obtained Arts Council funding to rent the theatre, which became the Arts Theatre, opening in October 1945 with H.E. Bates's ***Day of Glory***. Renamed the Playhouse and reopened in July 1953, the theatre served Salisbury for over 20 years until a new Playhouse was opened on the site of the old maltings in November 1976 by Sir Alec Guinness. It provides the city and its environs with an imaginative and catholic repertoire, from Shakespeare and Webster to Stoppard and Ionesco. Meanwhile, the New Picture House, by now renamed the Odeon, was acquired by the City Council in 1962 as a memorial to the Allied victory in World War Two. As the City Hall it has provided a venue for acts ranging from Cliff Richard and the Beatles, to the Syd Lawrence Orchestra and Rosemary Squires. The first of the city's purpose-built cinemas, the Regal, is today a bingo and social club.

Libraries

Since the Enlightenment, Salisbury has been a city of letters, and libraries have been at the heart of the city's intellectual life. The earliest circulating library in Salisbury was in operation by 1738, run jointly by Samuel Fancourt and Edward Easton, and commercial and institutional circulating libraries continued to operate until well after World War Two. The commercial libraries were usually run as offshoots from bookselling and publishing businesses, the earliest of these being that of Easton, who split off from Fancourt's venture. In the 1790s there were three circulating libraries; by 1830 there were seven circulating libraries and three subscription libraries. In the 19th century, libraries came to be provided by the Mechanics' Institutes – in Salisbury's case in 1833, when its library

Salisbury Library's first learning access point. On the day of its opening, 29 July 2000, Jad Bienek, reference librarian, demonstrates the system to an enquirer, while Mayor Steve Fear accesses the Internet.

was established as the Mechanics' Institution itself was set up. The Literary and Scientific Institution, within a year of its foundation in 1849, had 556 volumes in its library, of which 92 were donations. The following year the Public Libraries Act was passed, but it was not adopted by Salisbury until 1890. The first city library was in Endless Street, but 15 years later, owing to the generosity of the Scots-born American industrialist Andrew Carnegie, Salisbury gained its first purpose-built library in Chipper Lane, which was to serve it until October 1975, when new premises were opened on the site of the Market House, behind Strapp's three-bay façade of Bath stone. Over the years, facilities have expanded enormously, from stock the patrons of the private libraries would have recognised to resources unimaginable to readers and librarians whose careers began even 30 years ago, such as CDs, CD-ROMs and DVDs and access to the internet from a multi-terminal learning access point. From the last years of the Chipper Lane library to the present time the children's library, under Jo Little's direction, has been an internationally admired and locally cherished centre of excellence.

Exhibition spaces

The one thing Salisbury does not possess is a free-standing dedicated art gallery. In 1913 the Edwin Young Gallery was opened next door to the city library, to display its founder's gift of 845 watercolours of the city and environs. Its endowment was insufficient to meet its running costs, and it came to be run as part of the library. On the transfer of library services to the County

Edwin Young gave funds for a gallery for the exhibition of his collection of watercolours of pastoral landscapes, genre scenes and streetscapes: (top) the dedication inscription; (middle and bottom) typical examples of his work: a farmyard at Harnham, the cathedral across the water meadows.

Council, and the move to the Market House site in 1975, the commitment to the figurative arts was maintained with the dedication of three (later four) gallery spaces, including one each for the Young Collection and that endowed by the crime novelist John Creasey. Under the imaginative curatorship of Monte Little, Annette Ratuszniak, Peter Mason and Peter Riley, the galleries remain the heart of the city's fine art exhibition space. Elsewhere, the museum and the Mediaeval Hall in the Close, the Salisbury Arts Centre, the foyers of the Playhouse, the City Hall and the District Hospital and the various commercial galleries offer manifold opportunities for the enjoyment of art, and for a fortnight every year the city becomes its own arts centre and museum, with the festival. The first Festival of the Arts took place in 1967, and has been held every year since 1973. High points in recent years have been the open-air and gallery exhibitions curated by Annette Ratuszniak, 'Elisabeth Frink: a certain unexpectedness' (1997), 'The shape of the century' (1999) and 'In praise of trees' (2002). Even when the festival is not running, Salisbury manages to maintain something of a festival atmosphere throughout the year, because, in addition to exhibitions, concerts, recitals and stage productions, the Arts Centre, opened in 1975 in St Edmund's Church after it was declared redundant as a place of worship, stages events of all kinds and to suit every taste.

Salisbury as its own exhibition space. (Above) Annette Ratuszniak, curator of 'Elisabeth Frink: a certain unexpectedness', the Salisbury Festival exhibition in 1997; (right) Frink head, cathedral cloisters; (bottom) Giles Penny, 'man with open arms' in the Market Place, 'The shape of the century', Salisbury Festival exhibition, 1999.

Sports

One of the earliest references to sporting activity describes how, in March 1583, 'ther was a race runned with horses at the Fursyes, three myles from Harnem Hyll', with a prize of a gold bell worth more than £50. It was an aristocratic event, with the Earls of Warwick, Pembroke and Essex, and Sir Walter Hungerford and Sir John Danvers as participants, and the Earl of Cumberland the winner. Salisbury retains its place in the racing calendar to this day. By the late 19th century there was a wide range of sporting activities, many of which have an unbroken history to date. They include the Old Sarum Archers, founded in 1791, and the South Wilts Cricket Club, sufficiently well established by 1854 to play against an All-England team in June of that year, and to win by three runs. A local football league competing for the Salisbury and District Football Challenge Cup, was instituted in 1892, and the Cycling and Athletic Club in 1885, growing to a membership of 300 by 1897.

The City's first proper open-air swimming pool was opened in 1875, near the Market House, followed by another in the early 1930s, itself to be succeeded by a covered swimming pool near the Council House in 1976, and, in August 2002 by new facilities at the Leisure Centre, where, with archery practice at the butts after church in the 16th century, Salisbury's sporting life may be said to have begun. Today there are several hundred clubs, societies and forums for activities ranging from bonsai to battle re-enactment in Salisbury and the surrounding area, and the District Council has a sport and leisure policy to promote and maintain sporting facilities and initiatives throughout the District.

Epilogue: John Hall's dream

AT THE start of the 21st century, many of Salisbury's challenges are common throughout the prosperous south of England, and the key to maintaining its distinctive identity must lie in meeting those challenges without compromising that identity. But the authority which has that burden of duty is not that which, in one form or another, has guarded the city and its people for the first seven and a half centuries of its life, for in 1974, with local government reorganisation, the city disappeared, subsumed into an authority with command of 248,123 acres of south Wiltshire, and taking on the roles of the former rural and urban district councils. In many respects the new authority is better placed to guard the city's interests than before: responsibilities for trading standards, public health, highways and libraries, for example, now rest with the county or the NHS: the District Council, to that extent a more specialised

The city's growth in aerial photographs shortly after World War Two.

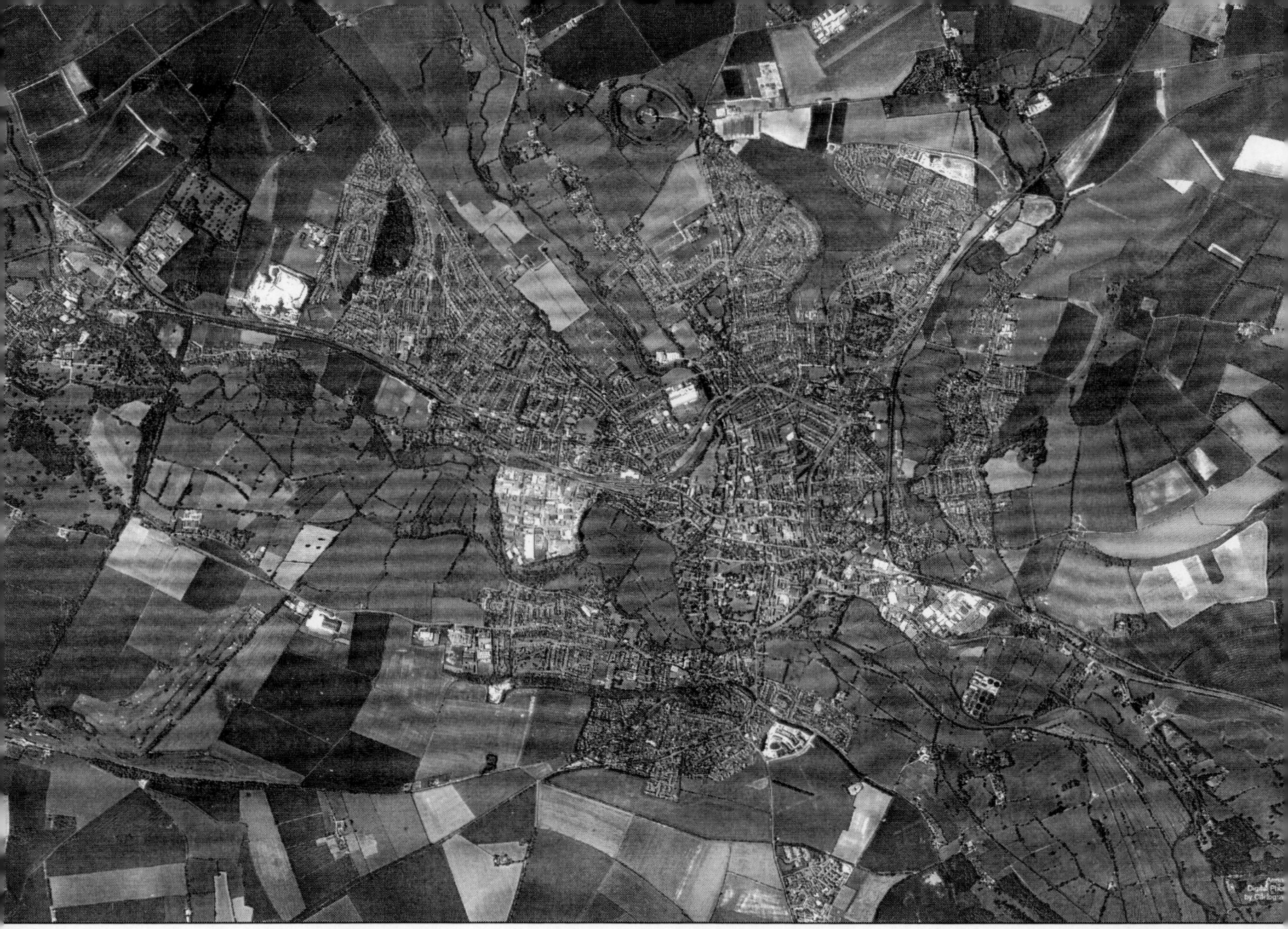

On 18 June 2000, taken by Cartographical Surveys Ltd. This photograph was Salisbury Library's Millennium Project, conceived and undertaken by Jad Bienek, Salisbury's reference librarian from 1998 to 2001. Sponsorship was raised from local businesses and from individuals, both local and visitors.

organisation, is able to take a more holistic and wide-ranging approach to the challenges facing Salisbury.

The sphere of transport remains problematic, and in the wake of the cancellation of the by-pass project, the interested parties have been forced to consider the problems anew. On the judgement that Salisbury's traffic problems are mainly local, the resulting solutions fall into two main categories. The first is relief of traffic congestion on the road, where existing roads are inadequate. Proposals within the Salisbury Transport Study include a number of local schemes, including a relief road to the south and west of Harnham, and access to the Churchfields Industrial Estate. The second is management of the traffic coming into Salisbury, and there has been a shift away from the idea of providing high-density parking in the city centre to limiting incoming traffic. The city's first park-and-ride scheme, at the Beehive site off the Castle Road came into effect in April 2001, and land has been acquired for one on

The staff of Salisbury Library at the unveiling of the photograph in March 2001.

the Downton Road: others are under consideration for the London and Southampton Roads. And yet the spectre of the strategic Southampton-Bristol route cannot be dismissed. One of the reasons for the by-pass as originally planned was to remove accident black

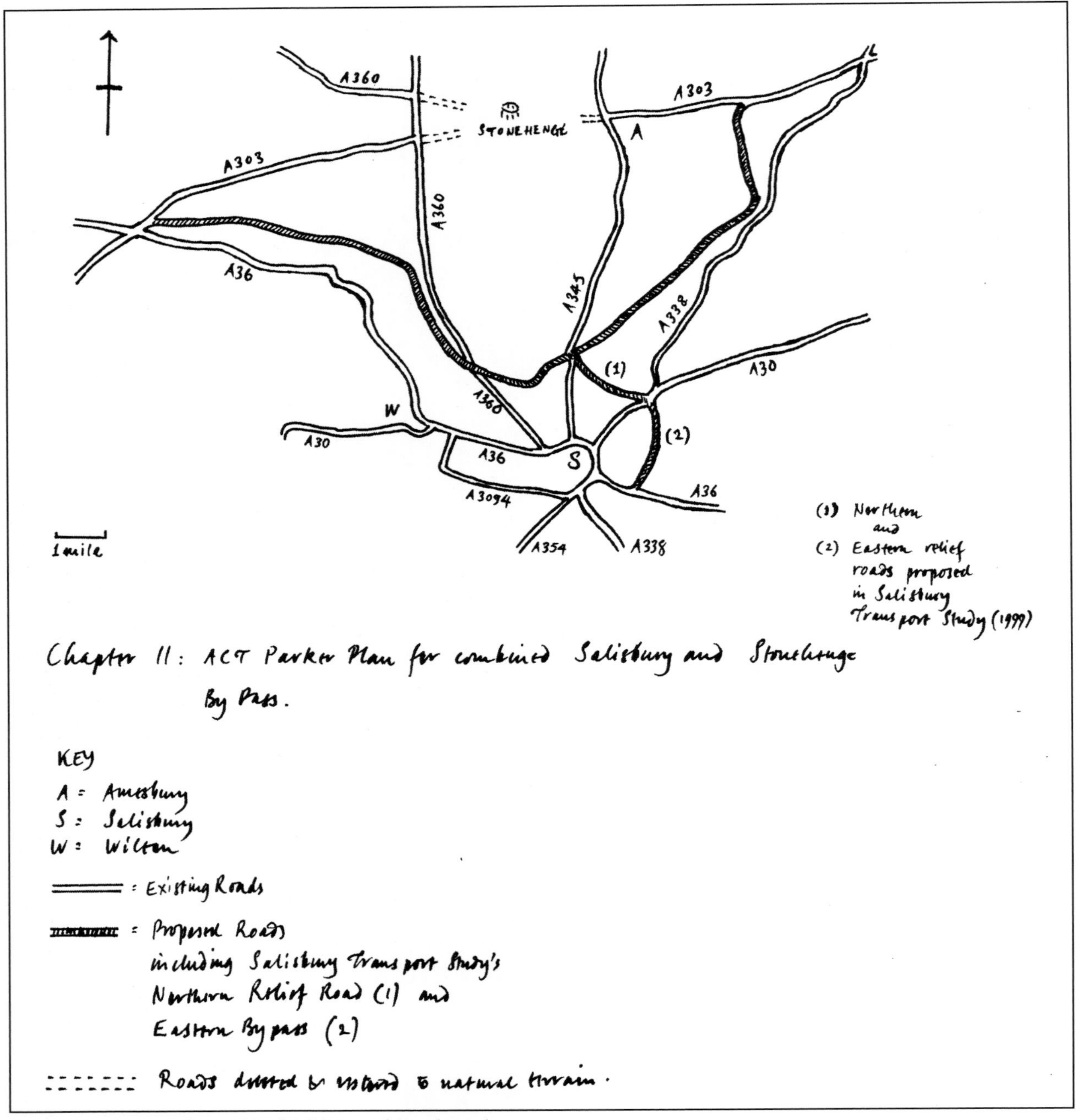

ACT Parker Plan route for combined Salisbury and Stonehenge by-pass.

spots and environmental degradation in the Wylye Valley, and later by-pass proposals include the building of new roads north and east of the city and upgrading the A360. Meanwhile, the Government is committed to the closure of the roads around Stonehenge, seven miles north of Salisbury, and the creation of a by-pass on the A303, using a 1½-mile tunnel. The Stonehenge Alliance argues for a longer bored tunnel on archaeological and environmental grounds, while other local commentators have observed that the line of the proposed short tunnel could create new accident black spots. The most radical and cost-effective solution, devised by Lt-Col. Graham Parker and endorsed by the Association of Council Taxpayers, involves bringing the Stonehenge by-pass route far enough south to serve as a by-pass for Salisbury and combining it with routes

The new Waitrose superstore. When the plans for the redevelopment of the Cattle Market Site were unveiled in 1994, the headline in the ***Salisbury Journal*** screamed 'Monstrosity', and the view of Old Sarum from the cathedral tower will never be the same. Yet the Waitrose shop has the great merit of offering the product range and services of an out-of-town superstore while being within easy reach of the north of the city. As an indication of present-day priorities it is interesting to note that at 55,000sq ft it has a floor area 25% larger than the cathedral's.

proposed in the Salisbury Transport Study. By not tunnelling the route, the additional length would cost far less than the proposed scheme, and, in effect, provide a full by-pass for Salisbury at marginal, if any, cost. If the arguments for a Salisbury by-pass are accepted, then the ACT scheme deserves at least the same consideration as the 50-year-old shibboleth of the southern by-pass route.

As for the city, it has met the challenges of the late 20th century with no little success. Like any market town and tourist centre at the centre of a communications network, Salisbury has attracted the attention of the major retailers in the last half-century, with the alleged consequence that it looks like any other southern market town. In fact, the presence of multiples, of all kinds, has grown only by about 30 per cent over the last 30 years. What makes their presence more obvious is the fact that in some cases – Marks and

Distinctive local businesses include (left) Pennyfarthing Tools, established 1993, and a Mecca for engineers, craftsmen and hobbyists from around the world; and (right) Perkins Motor Accessories, where the Perkinses offered a personal service to the DIY motorist for 40 years.

Distinction of a different kind can be found on the city's outskirts: the Autechnique showroom on the London Road was honoured in 1995 by Salisbury District Council with an award for its contribution to the built environment.

From time to time Salisbury holds a French market.

Flowers at the Guildhall following the death of Diana, Princess of Wales on 31 August 1997.

Spencer, Boots and Tesco, for example – they have combined premises: they are simply bigger than they were. Many of the multiples sell information – banks, building societies and estate agents – which limits their appeal to the visitor, but their high-value business enables them to afford to trade in the city centre in Salisbury as elsewhere. The sector enjoying the most significant growth is probably the charity shops, which have grown from one to about a dozen over the last 30 years. In fact, Salisbury's central business district is compact enough that the specialist shops, which tend to be on the periphery in any town, are still within easy walking distance of the Market Place. The pedestrianisation of much of the city centre in March 1998, and traffic management elsewhere in favour of people has given Salisbury back to its own and to its visitors. At the

Light industry to city centre housing. Where light industry has been discontinued, the brownfield site can lend itself well to residential development, as in the case of (above) the Gibbs, Mew brewery in Gigant Street, photographed in the 1980s, replaced by (below) Charter Court, dating from the turn of the millennium The Anchor Tap public house is currently being redeveloped.

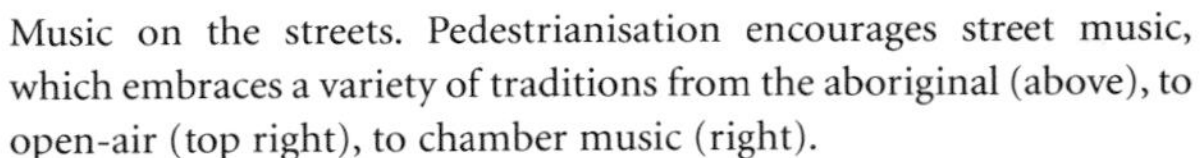

Music on the streets. Pedestrianisation encourages street music, which embraces a variety of traditions from the aboriginal (above), to open-air (top right), to chamber music (right).

same time, Salisbury has succeeded in reinventing itself as somewhere to live. Its industries have not had a heavy impact on the environment, so its regeneration has lent itself well to housing developments, such as Archer's Court, the Infirmary, Three Cups and those in the eastern Chequers. In 1956, Arnold Hare wrote: 'John Halle, or any of his 15th-century contemporaries, would have had little difficulty in recognising the Salisbury of 1660 or 1790; at first sight that of 1956 would have seemed to them at best a dream, at worst a fantastic nightmare'. The care with which challenges have been met and change has been managed have undoubtedly tipped the balance in favour of the dream.

Floreat Sarisberia.

Part Two
Tours around Salisbury

Introduction

HAVING surveyed Salisbury's history from the earliest times, we are now in a position to consider the tangible evidence of the processes of change, both from illustrations made in the past and the city's buildings and streetscapes as they stand today. The main sources for the illustrations from times past are Francis Price, who illustrated his own book on Salisbury Cathedral, published in 1753; Frederick Mackenzie, who illustrated John Britton's ***History and antiquities of the Cathedral Church of Salisbury*** (1814); William Henry Bartlett, who illustrated John Britton's ***Picturesque antiquities of the English cities*** (1829); John Fisher, who illustrated Peter Hall's ***Picturesque memorials of Salisbury*** (1834); Edwin Young and the photographers whose work appears in the Lovibond Collection.

Francis Price was an architect and had already published a key work, ***The British Carpenter, or a Treatise on Carpentry,*** when in 1734 he was appointed Surveyor to the Cathedral and Clerk of Works to the Dean and Chapter. From his appointment until his death he oversaw an extensive programme of repairs to the cathedral, and published the earliest account of the cathedral, its design and structure, which appeared in the year of his death, 1753.

John Britton (1771–1857) was a pivotal figure both as a topographical writer and as the moving force behind what Richard Hatchwell has described as the reformation in English topographical illustration of the early 19th century. His education was sketchy in the extreme, and his achievement is thus all the more remarkable. His career as a topographical writer began with Wheble's commission to write ***The beauties of Wiltshire,*** followed by ***The beauties of England and Wales,*** which he undertook with his friend Edward Brayley. What was revolutionary about their writing was that it was based both on the authorities of the past – Camden and Cox – and also on their own very extensive fieldwork. The first five volumes entailed 3,500 miles of travel. For this enormous undertaking (of which he was responsible for the text of six volumes), Britton gathered about him a group of artists whose names are a roll-call of the leading landscape artists of the early 19th century. They included W.H. Bartlett, Frederick Nash and Frederick Mackenzie, whose works are featured elsewhere in this book; also John Sell Cotman, John Buckler and J.M.W. Turner and, among engravers, the Le Keux brothers.

Britton's later works included ***The architectural antiquities of Great Britain*** (1805–1814, 4 vols), and, most ambitious of all, ***The cathedral antiquities of Great Britain*** (1814–1835, 14 vols), which began with his ***History and antiquities of the cathedral church of Salisbury.*** Engravings from both of these works appear in the following pages. Throughout this time and for the rest of his life Britton was engaged on other writing projects, and there are 87 items in the list of publications in his autobiography (1849). Prolific though Britton was, his livelihood was at times precarious, but it is a measure of the esteem in which he was held in cultured circles that efforts were made to secure him a reliable income. His friends and admirers presented him with £1,000 on his 74th birthday, in 1845, to which he responded by compiling his autobiography, and Disraeli secured him a civil list pension. Another source of income was the sale of his library, either individual volumes, or as tranches. It was the sale of one such, prefaced by the expressed hope of it remaining as a discrete Wiltshire collection, which led to the foundation of the Wiltshire Archaeological and Natural History Society. Britton also proposed the founding of a society, 'The Guardian of National Antiquities' which anticipated by many decades the founding of the National Trust.

The Revd Peter Hall (1803–1849) had a career dogged by misfortune: after five years' service he was dismissed from his first appointment, at St Edmund's Church, and only 18 months later did he secure another living. He wrote a number of topographical works on Hampshire and Wiltshire, mainly concentrating on the New Forest area, as well as liturgical treatises, of which he also edited a considerable quantity. His biographer in the ***Dictionary of National Biography*** remarks that 'His labours as editor and biographer are of little value, though his topographical works may be found useful.' Indeed: his topographical writing on Salisbury has a value far beyond that which anyone would have surmised at the time of its publication. The illustrations for the ***Picturesque memorials of Salisbury*** were undertaken mainly by John Fisher: they were to appear in many subsequent tourist guides to the city throughout the 19th century.

Edwin Young was born in 1831, the son of a cobbler who died when Edwin was young. His mother had to raise him and his seven siblings single-handed, and succeeded in establishing them all in business or public life. Young's career began with surveying for a local land agent, and by his early fifties he was able to retire in order to devote himself to painting and work for local charities. His paintings were exhibited at the Bath and West of England Society Show in 1866, and elsewhere subsequently, to critical acclaim. He died in 1913.

The Lovibond Collection arises from a commission by the City Council's Ancient Buildings Committee in November 1923 to two of its members, J.L. Lovibond and F. Watson, to record ancient buildings and those of picturesque value. Joseph Locke Lovibond (1876–1954) was the nephew and godson of Joseph Williams Lovibond, Mayor of Salisbury, and assumed the running of the Salisbury operation of the family brewing business on his uncle's death in 1918. The photography carried out at the time and subsequently (the survey continued for at least 10 years) was the work of Reginald William Harding, proprietor of the Royal Studio at 38 High Street from the turn of the century until at least 1944. Many much earlier photographs were also incorporated into the collection.

A decision was taken to repeat the exercise just after the war, but no action appears to have resulted. The next full photographic survey of the city was undertaken on the initiative of Monte Little as Salisbury Divisional Librarian, Wiltshire Library and Museum Service. The photography was by Maurice Haselgrove (1979–80) and John Lawrence (1981–92). The most recent survey was undertaken between 1999 and 2000 as a millennium project by the Salisbury Camera Club.

The first five tours begin on the outskirts of the city, starting from Castle Street in the north and proceeding clockwise to Fisherton Street. All move inwards towards the city centre. The sixth starts in the Maltings and ends at the High Street Gate of the Close, the seventh surveys the Close and the eighth notes some interesting buildings and scenes in the city's environs.

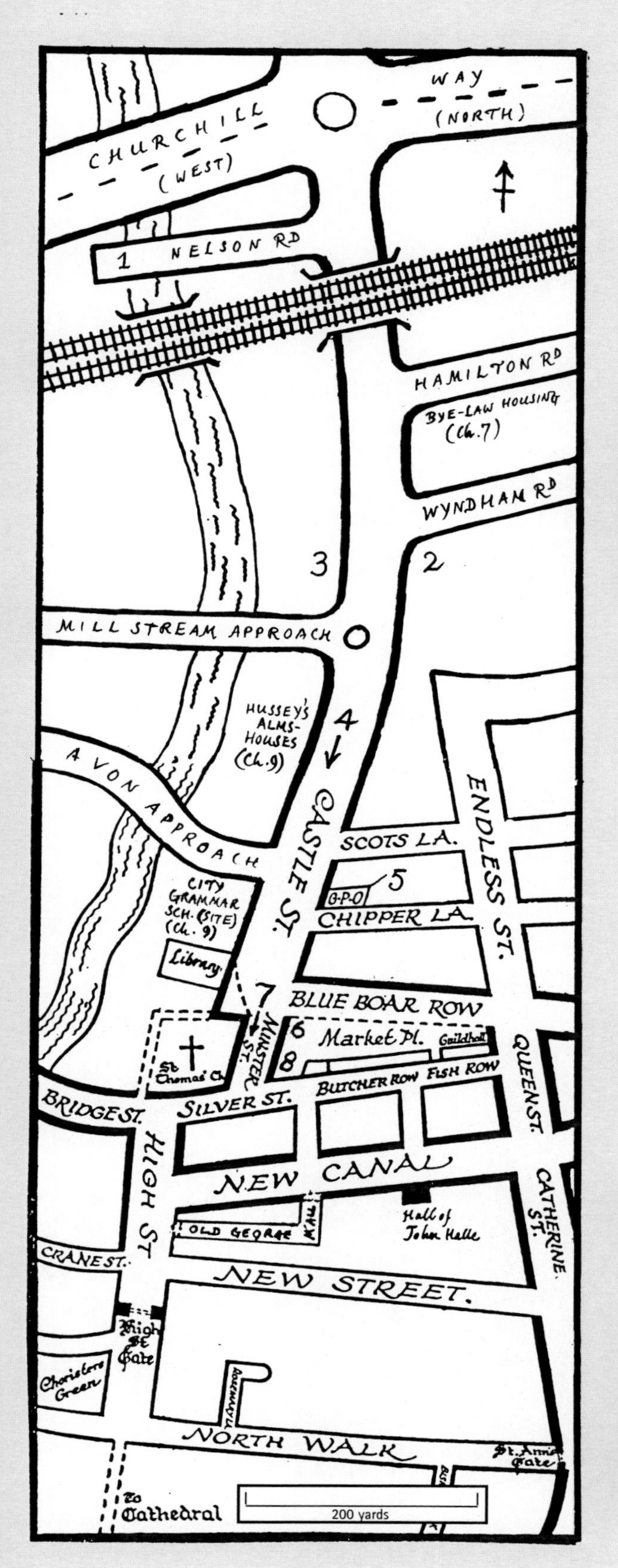

Tour 1
Nelson Road to Minster Street

1. Nelson Road

Nelson Road: Tollgate. In the early years of the last century, there was no direct route from the north end of Castle Road to the suburbs north of Fisherton Street and east of the Devizes Road. Thomas Scamell acquired the railway bridge when it was too small to carry the necessary volume of traffic, and rebuilt it to cross the Avon at the end of Nelson Road, giving access onto his private road heading towards the west end of Fisherton Street. The toll payable was initially 1d for pedestrians, reduced subsequently to ½d and dropped altogether by 1931.

Cul-de-sac, 2002.

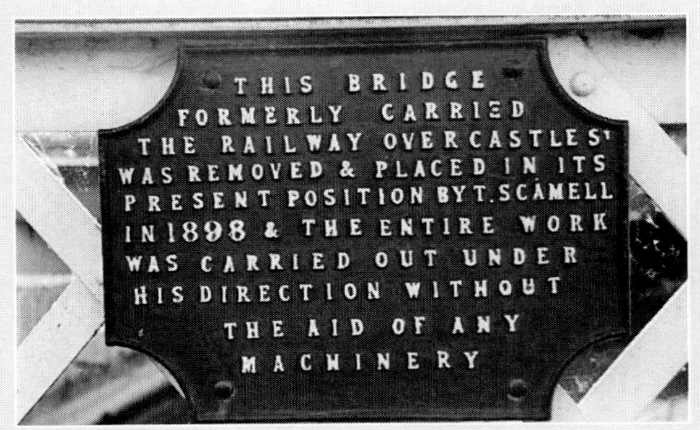

Plate on bridge over the Avon.

2. Corner of Wyndham Road

194 Castle Street, home of Richard Dear, wine and spirit merchant in 1897.

Castle Street Toyota Garage, 2002.

3. The Rising Sun

The Rising Sun Inn, 1908.

Archers Court, a recent development of retirement flats by McCarthy and Stone plc, 2002.

4. Castle Street at the Site of the City Gate

General view south towards the cathedral, W.H. Bartlett, 1829.

The same view, 2002.

Weathered coat of arms from the Castle Gate, now on side of Hussey's Almshouses.

5. The Post Office

Corner of Chipper Lane, before 1905, when the site had been acquired for the Post Office.

The Post Office, 2002.

6. The Corner of Minster Street and the Market Place

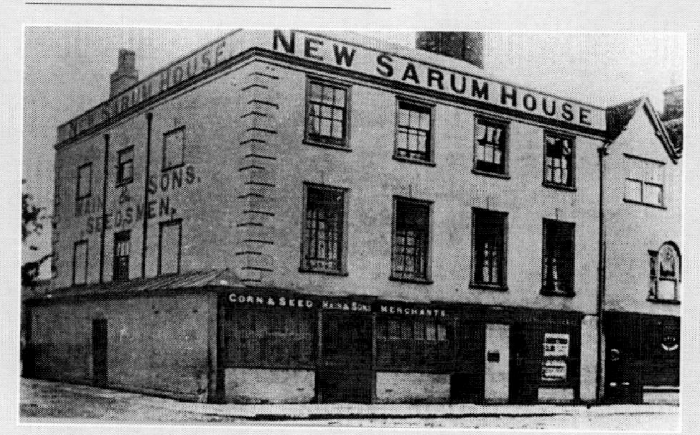

As Main's, seed merchant's premises.

New Sarum House, built for Main's, now the Portman Building Society, 2002.

MASTERS

(Previous page) General view south towards Silver Street, with the cathedral tower and spire in the background, and showing the watercourse. Of the traders' names legible in this view, only 'Langharm' may perhaps be identified with William Lanham, tobacconist and clothes dealer in Silver Street, listed in contemporary directories, while the Haunch of Venison Inn and Carter's, jewellers (where the name 'Masters' can be read) were well established when this scene was recorded.

7. Minster Street

The same view, 2002. The gable bracket on the left, and the properties on the right – Wynchestre's house, The Haunch of Venison and Carter's – are unchanged. The major loss to the view is the building of Marks and Spencer (now Boots), which obscures all but the top 90-odd feet of the cathedral spire.

8. Poultry Cross

View from the corner of Minster Street, early 1930s.

The same view, 2002.

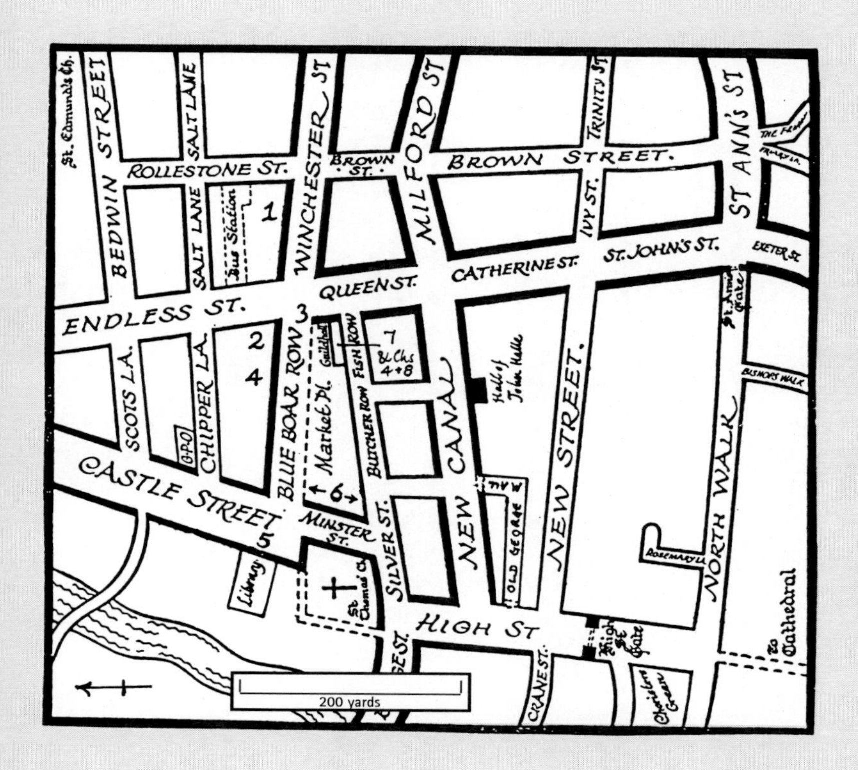

Tour 2

Winchester Street to the Market Place

1. North Side of Winchester Street, Looking West

Before the war.

2002: since the first photograph was taken, the Salisbury and District Co-operative Society built new premises east of the Three Swans Inn, and in turn these have been taken over by McDonalds.

2. East Corner of Blue Boar Row and Endless Street

In the 1920s this plot, recorded in mediaeval records as Nugge's corner, was occupied by a jeweller and watchmaker, then by a garage.

Today, the premises are a café below and an internet café above, 2002.

3. North-east Corner of the Market Place

In the mid-19th century, the property on the corner of Winchester Street and Queen Street was a chemist's, but in 1878 became the offices of Pinckney's Bank, the new building incorporating timbers from the Saracen's Head inn in Blue Boar Row.

In 2002, Pinckney's bank has long gone, but its offices remain as Cross Keys House.

4. Blue Boar Row: Higgins the Chemist's

Towards the west end of Blue Boar Row there was a pharmacy which had traded since 1802 under the proprietorship of Robert Squarey. The business subsequently passed into the hands of C.W. Higgins, and had a frontage inspired – however distantly – by Inigo Jones's New Covent Garden.

Illustration of New Covent Garden, detail, from Campbell's ***Vitruvius Britannicus*** (1717).

No.47 Blue Boar Row, still a chemist's, doubtless much lighter and airier to work in and to visit.

5. The Cheese Market and the Market House

The Maidenhead Inn, dating from the 15th century, and rebuilt in 1769, from a photograph before 1859, when the Market House was built.

The Market House, a conjectural view, late 1850s. The family firm of Prangley – father and sons – were chemists, specialising in agricultural chemicals and artificial fertilisers, later branching out into oil-cake, corn and seed. They traded from about 1830 until the late 1880s; their premises' present name (see below) dates from only the late 1920s.

Salisbury Library and Galleries, 2002.

6. Oatmeal Row and St Thomas's Church

An early 20th-century postcard view, showing St Thomas's Church belfry.

The same view, 2002, partially obscured by the lime trees planted to mark Queen Victoria's Golden Jubilee, 1887.

7. The Guildhall

As it first looked in 1795: a lithograph published in Benson and Hatcher's ***Old and New Sarum***, 1843.

As it looks today, without the western colonnade, and the northern colonnade moved forward of the original building line.

Tour 3

Milford Street to New Canal

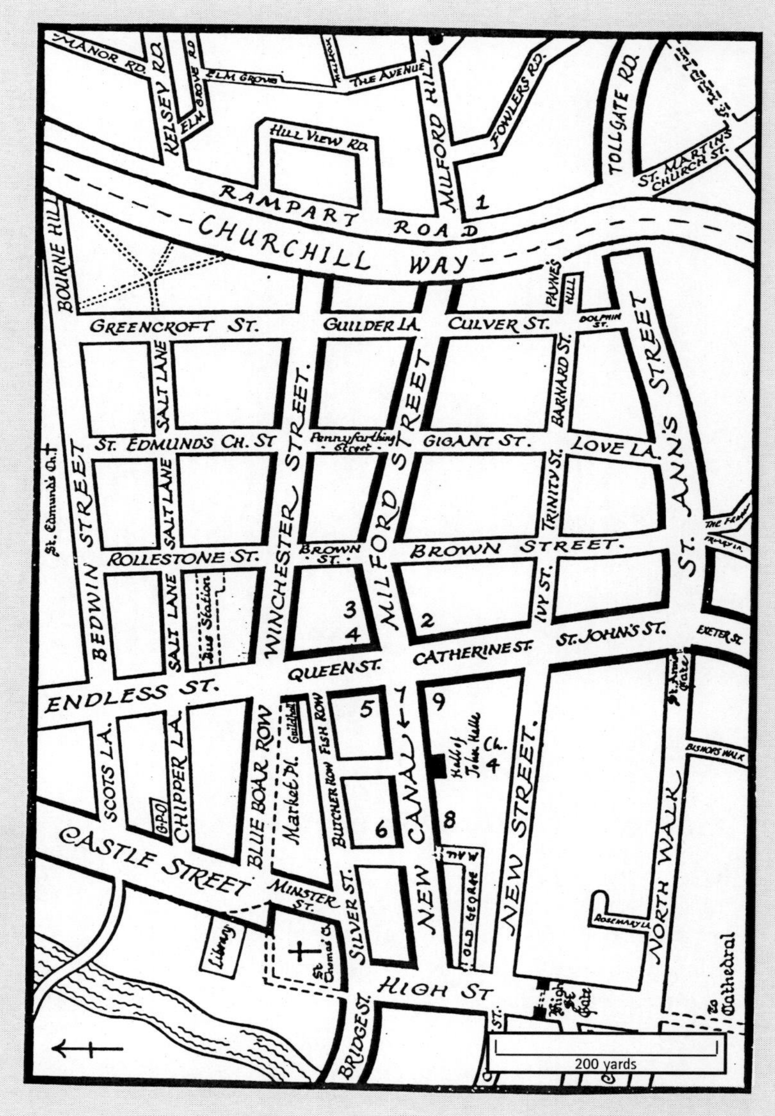

1. 'Shakespeare Scene': the top end of Milford Street

As shown and as so named in Hall's *Picturesque memorials*, 1834. Immediately left of the timber-framed building is the London Road.

The timber-framed building was No.88 Milford Street, and was demolished to make way for Churchill Way East in 1972.

All that remains of Hall's view today: even these properties have undergone some alteration.

2. Corner of Milford Street and Catherine Street

Apart from the colour of the corner premises and the wording of the Red Lion Hotel's name board, the scene is virtually the same today.

3. The Cathedral Hotel

Opposite the Red Lion is the Cathedral Hotel. Until the early years of the last century the hotel had only two storeys.

An engraved bill-head, showing the premises of H. Ward, pastry-cook and confectioner, 1872, who was succeeded by Fielder and Son before the premises became the Cathedral Hotel.

The Cathedral Hotel today.

4. Corner of Milford Street and Queen Street

As Wilkes and Son, ironmongers, at around 1900: the business was trading here for about 100 years up to the late 1920s.

Today, completely redeveloped.

5. Corner of New Canal and Queen Street

Other than by the presence of the balconettes facing onto New Canal and the absence of the policeman on point duty, the scene is little changed from 1928, when this photograph was probably taken.

6. North-West Corner of New Canal

In the 1920s.

In 2002.

7. General View West down New Canal

At the turn of the 20th century.

8. The Post Office

Before the move to Chipper Lane, late 19th/early 20th century.

As the New Canal entrance to Marks and Spencer, 2002.

9. Corner of New Canal and Catherine Street

Bloom's site as redeveloped, now home to a tattoo shop, Laura Ashley and so on, 2002.

Bloom's was a local family firm of tailors and outfitters, trading from the late 19th to the late 20th century, so successfully that they were able to redevelop this site.

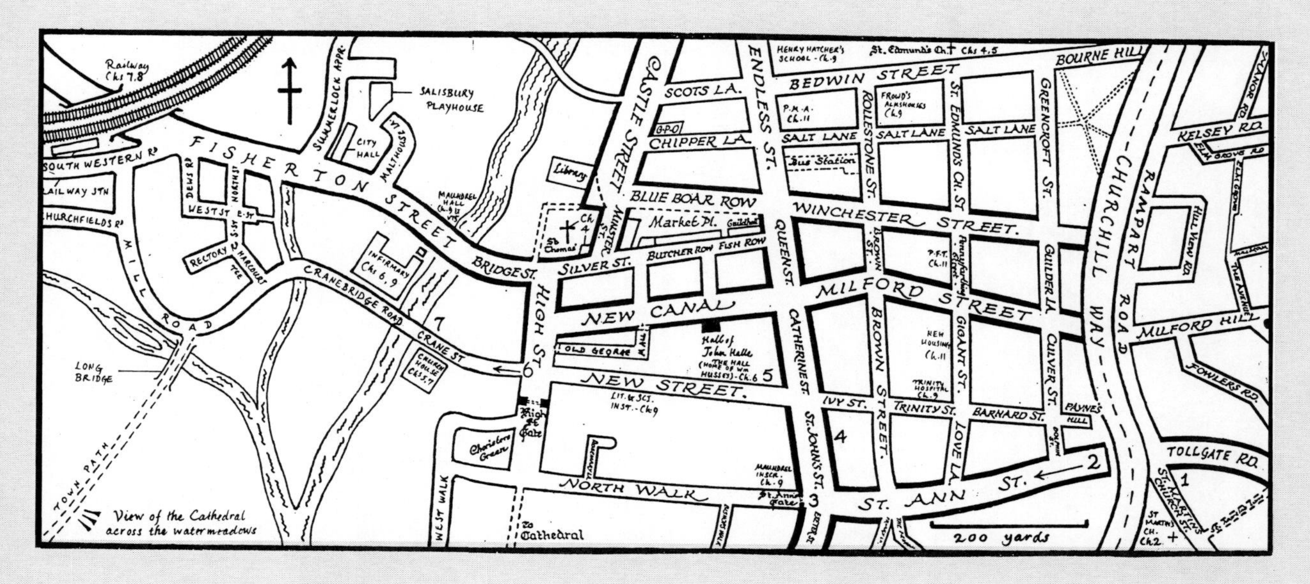

TOUR 4
ST ANN STREET TO THE TOWN PATH

1. The Tollgate Inn

As the New Inn in 1895.

As the Tollgate Inn in 2002. The major difference is the presence of the ring road.

2. St Ann Street

View up St Ann Street, 2002. (Compare with the frontispiece, from Hall's ***Picturesque memorials***, 1834.)

Moorland House, before the war. Visible at the left of the view in Hall's ***Picturesque memorials***, it was demolished in 1964 to make way for Churchill Way East.

3. St Ann's Gate

As depicted in Hall's ***Picturesque memorials***, 1834, and unchanged today except for street furniture.

4. The King's Arms

As depicted in an engraving by Charles Kimber, and readily recognisable today.

5. Corner of New Street and Catherine Street

As the home of Wessex Motors, before the war. Just visible at the left is The Hall, home of William Hussey, alderman and MP for the city in the reign of George III.

Today – office premises.

6. General View of Crane Street

As depicted in Hall's ***Picturesque memorials***, 1834.

Today: the major difference is in the remodelling of the façade of No.91 Crane Street.

7. Crane Bridge and the Workhouse

As depicted in a watercolour by Edwin Young, and readily recognisable today.

As the scene is today, 2002.

8. The Cathedral from the Town Path

A few yards on from Crane Bridge lies the Town Path, a causeway over the water meadows. From here is to be seen the view of Salisbury Cathedral, voted the best view in Britain in a poll of readers of ***Country Life***, published 25 July 2002.

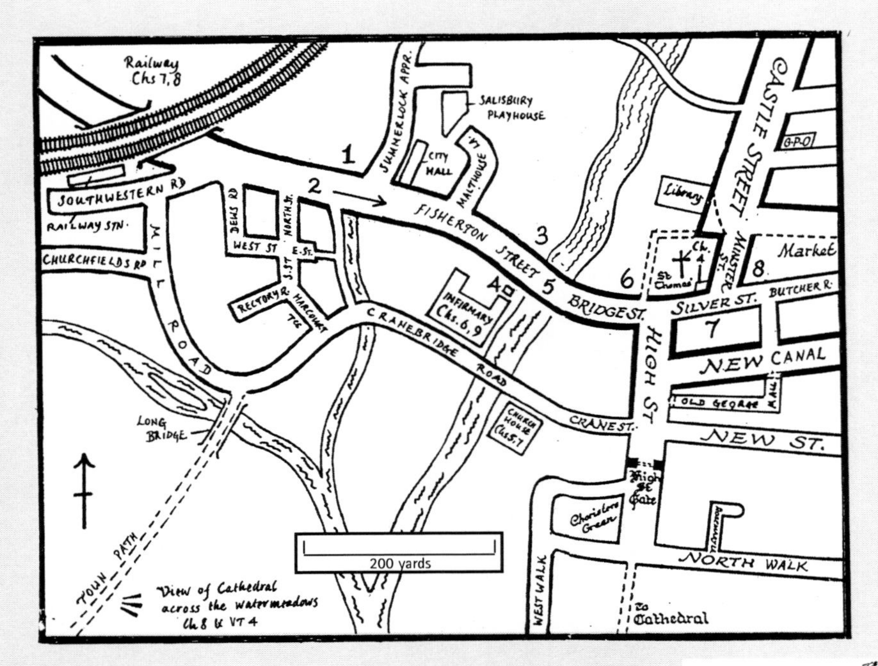

Tour 5 From Fisherton Street to the Poultry Cross

1. Summerlock Bridge

At the time of the floods in 1852: this print is from the ***Illustrated London News***, which reported: 'The city of Salisbury has been recently visited with serious floods. All the lower parts of Fisherton have been from two to three feet under water. The inhabitants of several of the cottages were compelled to betake themselves, with their furniture, to the upper floors; and in many cases, considerable suffering and distress have been the result. Of course, the foot passenger traffic has been suspended, and horses and carts plied for hire between the Infirmary and the turnpike.'

From Hall's ***Picturesque memorials***, 1834, the double-span bridge, and the Waggon and Horses, on the north side of Fisherton Street.

In the era of photography, mid-19th century. The scene today is completely transformed, with Victorian buildings replacing the Waggon and Horses some time between 1867 and 1875, and a single, flat span replacing the humpbacked bridge in 1901.

2. General view up Fisherton Street

At the time of the floods in 1915.

After World War One, when Albany Ward's Picture House had replaced the Primitive Methodist chapel.

Today: Summerlock Approach runs by where the Picture House used to stand, its site now occupied by Multiyork Ltd.

3. The Maundrel Hall

Built in 1880 as a memorial to John Maundrel 'for evangelistic religious services', designed by Frederick Bath, shown here in a photograph dating from World War One. By World War Two it was being used as a services' club; latterly it was a branch of Argos.

Today the hall, under the name of Hogshead, satisfies physical rather than spiritual thirsts.

4. The Clock Tower

As the Infirmary took over the old gaol, by the late 19th century only this small corner remained by the bridge. This picture dates from before 1892.

In 1892 Dr John Roberts erected the clock tower as a memorial to his wife Arabellaa.

5. Fisherton Bridge

As depicted by Edwin Young in the late 19th century.

The present bridge, here shown under construction, was opened in 1961.

6. The Shoulder of Mutton

In business up to the 1960s, the Shoulder of Mutton was the first property on the north side of Bridge Street, facing onto St Thomas's Square.

Demolished, it provides a rare glimpse of the west end of St Thomas's Church.

Replaced by new buildings.

7. South side of Silver Street

Marks and Spencer, latterly Boots, 2002.

Hobden's, until the mid-1930s.

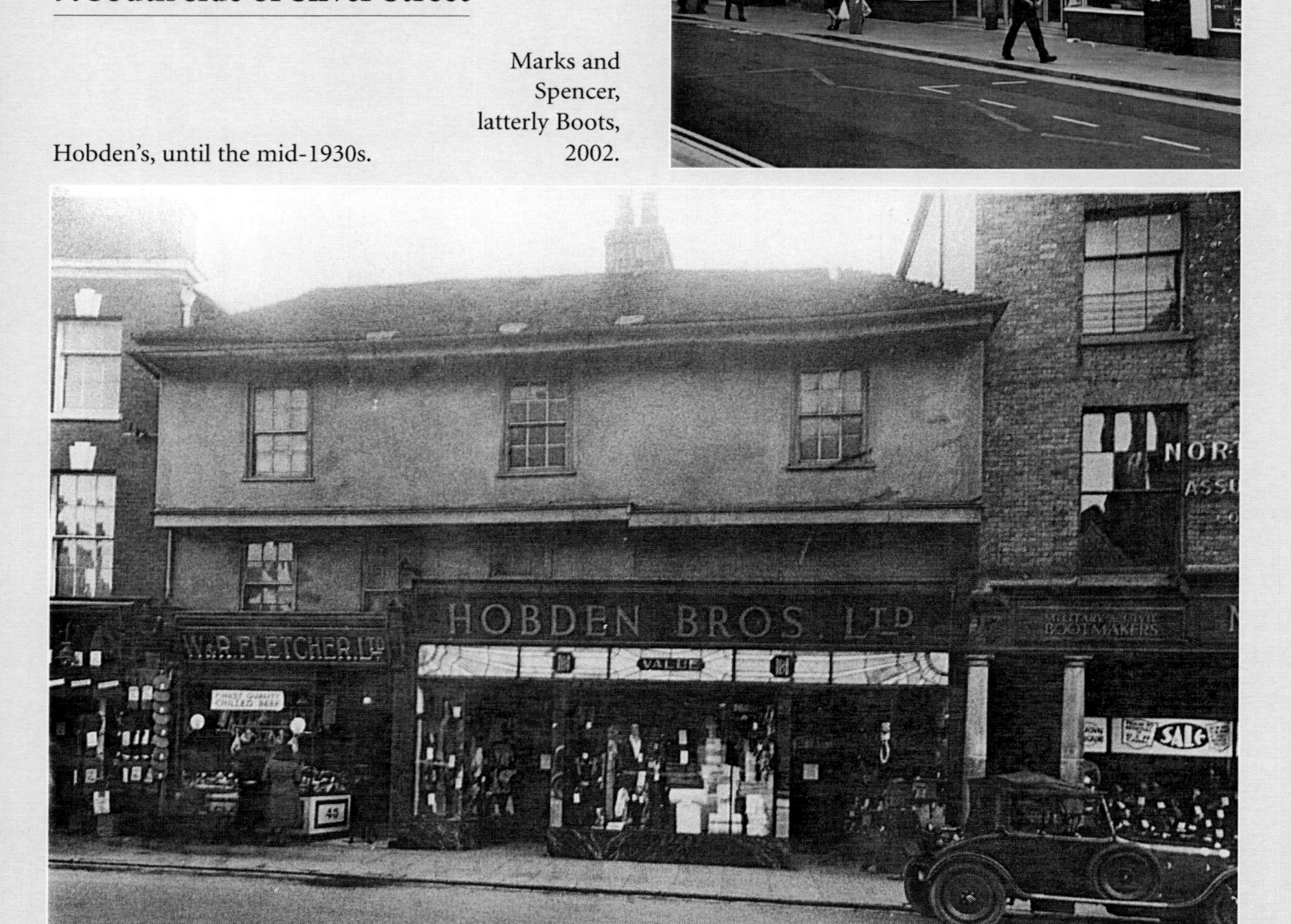

8. The Poultry Cross

As depicted in Hall's ***Picturesque memorials***, 1834. All is not what it seems, for the Poultry Cross in 1834 looked as illustrated (below), and the view above is conjectural, although it came to pass more or less exactly as depicted in 1853.

In 1834 this is what the Poultry Cross looked like, having been 'restored and beautified' in 1711.

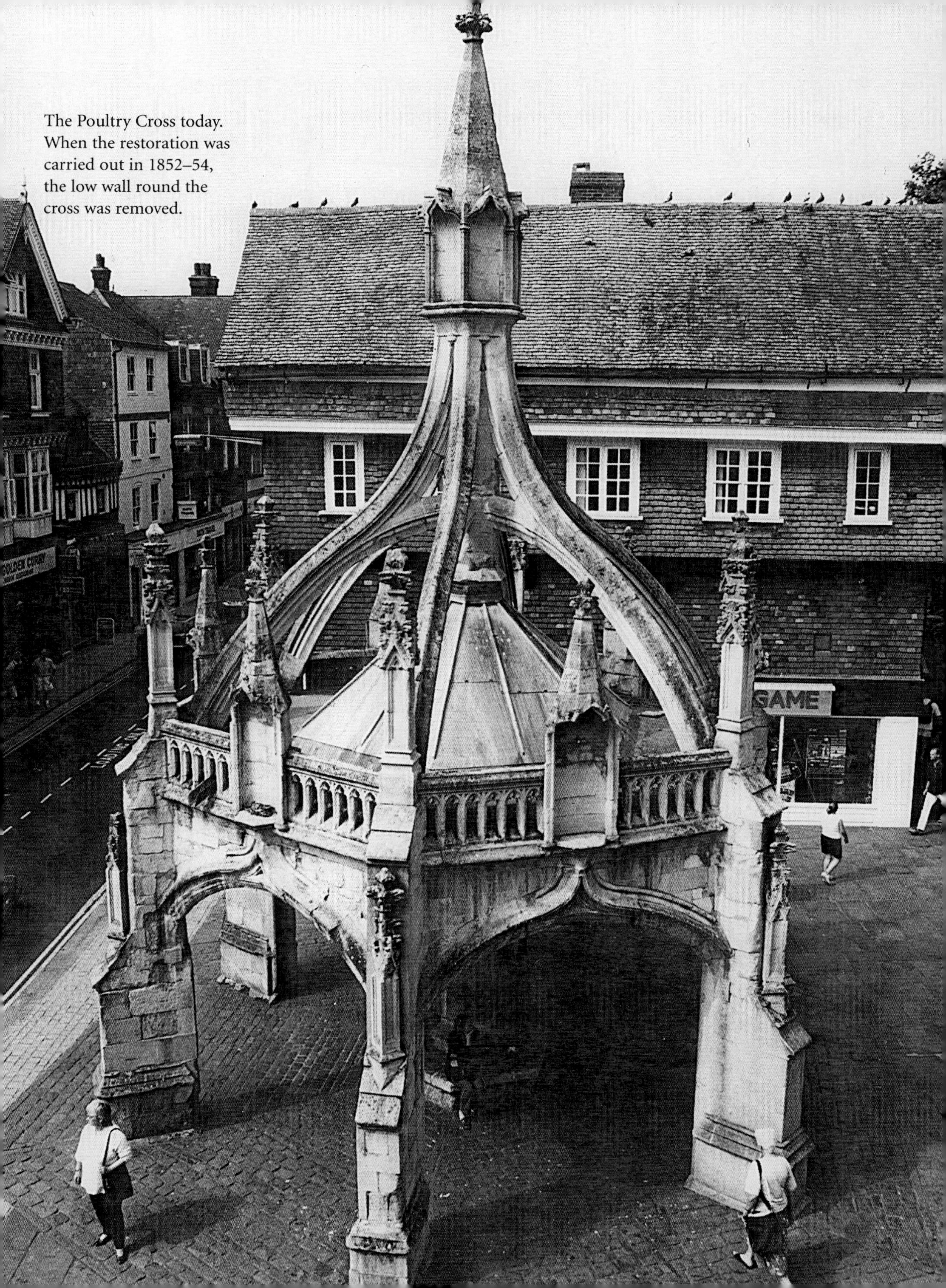

The Poultry Cross today. When the restoration was carried out in 1852–54, the low wall round the cross was removed.

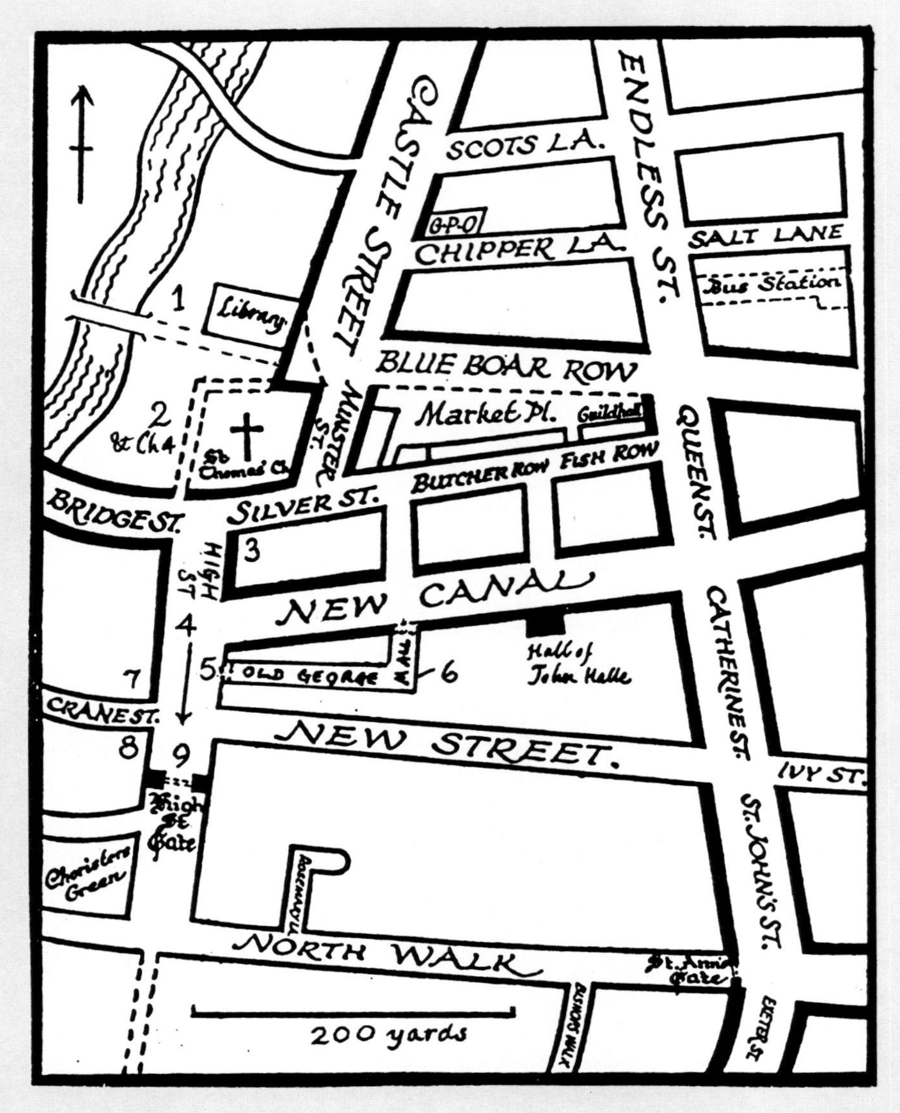

Tour 6

The Maltings to the High Street

1. The Maltings

The area beyond the Avon as it runs parallel to Castle Street has, with the exception of the city's first two swimming pools, generally been a working area. So it appears in this view of the river at the back of the Market House before its redevelopment.

The common feature is the bridge leading, today, into Market Walk. Other than that the area is transformed for leisure, with the library at the left, and for shopping.

2. St Thomas's Church

As depicted in Hall's ***Picturesque memorials***, 1834. Even at the time this view owed a little to imagination: 'Even from the spot selected for the annexed view, some liberty is unavoidably taken, to display the great West Window'.

With later building the view is almost completely obscured.

St Thomas's churchyard is little altered from the time when Edwin Young painted it in the late 19th century.

3. Corner of Silver Street and High Street

Snook's family butchers, before the war.

Today, as Lunn Poly.

When the building was being gutted in the late 1930s.

As depicted by W.H. Bartlett for Britton's ***Picturesque antiquities***, 1829. Apart from the conventional representation of the people, the horses and carts (for which W.H. Brooke was the artist) at half to two thirds life size, the cathedral has been increased in size, particularly the nave.

4. General View South, from the Old George Hotel to the High Street Gate

The pedestrianisation of the High Street in 1998 provides views more reminiscent of 19th-century engravings than has been possible throughout the 20th century.

5. The George Inn

Only when it was converted to a shopping precinct was its entrance opened out to the extent it had been as a coaching inn.

As depicted in Hall's ***Picturesque memorials***, 1834. By the time of this engraving it had not been an inn for over 70 years, which explains why its frontage is of shops, not that of a coaching inn. Mary Holly appears in ***Pigot's Directory***, 1830, as a stay-maker, and she is listed, aged 50+, sharing a house with two other stay-makers in the 1841 Census for the High Street. The stay-making business of Holly and Co., in the High Street, was still active in the 1850s. The George Inn subsequently reverted to its original purpose in 1858.

6. The Old George Mall

As built, with Marks and Spencer as the flagship store, 1969.

As redeveloped, 1995, with additional works being installed, 2002.

7. The Crown Hotel

Another old-established inn, dating from at least 1850, the Crown was diagonally opposite the George. As originally conceived it had the same roof height as its neighbours.

In the late 19th century it was greatly enlarged.

When the premises became retail/office space in the 1960s the roof height was brought back down to match the neighbouring properties.

8. Beach's Book Shop

Before ever it was a bookshop, the property on the south-west corner of the High Street and Crane Street junction was the premises of the family business of William, and later Reginald, Mullins, furniture and antique dealers.

Beach's Bookshop was trading for over 60 years, when it closed for the premises to become a restaurant.

The restaurant retained the name of the former trader for a year, before closing in 2002 for refurbishment and reopening as a branch of the Prezzo chain.

9. The High Street Gate

Other than the traders in the vicinity, the area south of the New Street/Crane Street junction has changed relatively little in almost 170 years, as this engraving from Hall's ***Picturesque memorials***, 1834, shows. Edward Fricker appears in Pigot's directory of 1842, and on the National Census a year before, with his wife, four children and a female servant.

The corresponding modern view.

Tour 7
The Close and the Cathedral

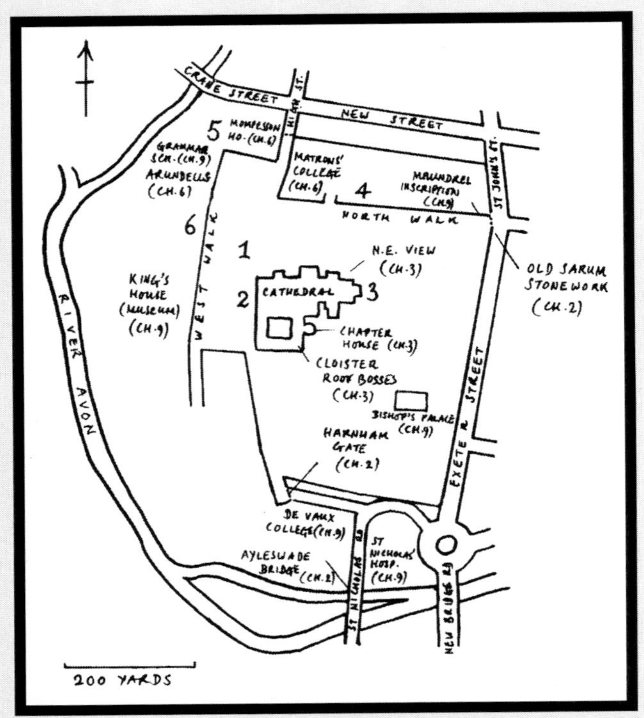

1. General View from the North-West

From Hall's ***Picturesque memorials***, 1834. On closer examination this view proves to be strangely anachronistic, perhaps idealised. The belfry, demolished over 40 years before, is restored, while the niches on the west front were not to be as well populated as shown here for another 40 years, with Scott's restoration. The eastern transept has been extended so as to be more visible from the engraver's presumed viewpoint.

A modern version of Hall's view is no longer possible with the avenue of trees which has lined the walk to the West Front for the last hundred years and more.

2. The West Front

As drawn by Nash for Dodsworth's ***Historical Account of the Episcopal See and Cathedral Church of Salisbury***, 1813, the façade is almost bare of statues.

Following the restorations by Scott in the 1860s and 1870s, and from 1995 to 2000, the West Front has almost 100 statues in place.

In this engraving from Britton's ***History and antiquities of the Cathedral Church of Salisbury***, 1814, the Hungerford and Beauchamp chantries are visible.

3. The East End

A modern photograph shows where they were and in fact how small they were.

4. Aula Le Stage

In Hall's ***Picturesque memorials***, 1834, this is illustrated by a wood engraving entitled 'Canon Bowles' house'. The canon was twice thwarted in love, and, already an accomplished poet, turned to writing verse for solace. He was also noted as an antiquary.

Bowles's house in the Close is Aula le Stage, and dates in part from the 13th century.

5. Hemingsby

In Hall's ***Picturesque memorials***, 1834, this is illustrated by a wood engraving entitled 'Court-yard at Chancellor Marsh's'. Marsh was Prebendary of Chute and Chancellor of the Diocese until his death in 1840.

Now two properties, numbered 56a and b, the building was bequeathed to the dean and chapter by Canon Alexander Hemingby in 1334. Altered in the 17th, 18th and 20th centuries, it was divided into two in 1950.

6. The North Canonry

As portrayed in Hall's ***Picturesque memorials***, 1834, and described as 'Houses of Canon Hume and James Lacy, Esq.', in Fisher's engraving it appears as a panorama of three properties, the North Canonry, Arundels and the Wardrobe. Hume was Thomas Henry Hume, son of Bishop John Hume (1766–1782), precentor 1774–1804 and a prebendary and canon residentiary who died in 1834. James Lacy is listed in Pigot's ***Directory*** of 1830 as Secretary to the Savings Bank in the High Street, and the agent for the Protector insurance society, with an office in New Street. The Savings Bank was eventually subsumed into Pinckney's Bank, featured above in Tour 2.

Because of the growth of the trees along the west walk, the nearest one can get to Fisher's vista is this view.

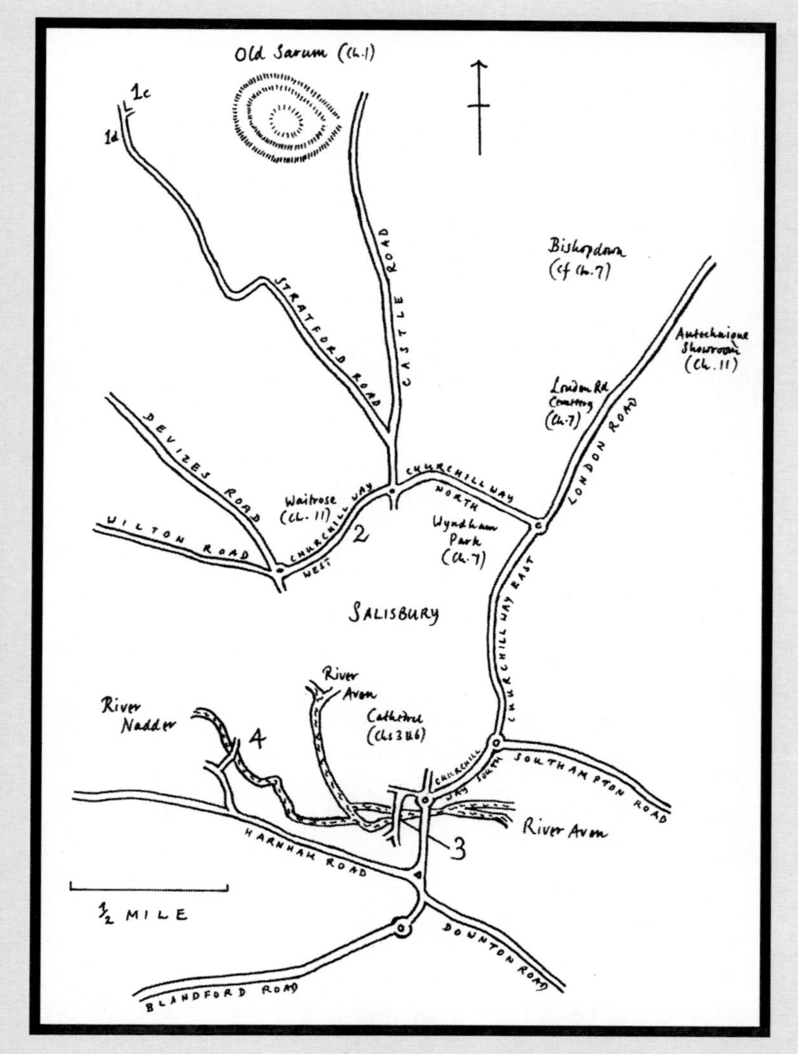

Tour 8

The Environs

1. Stratford sub Castle

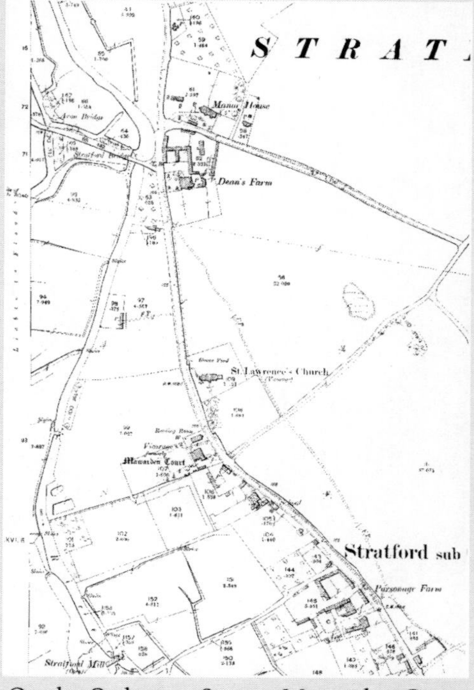

On the Ordnance Survey, Mawarden Court and the parish church of St Lawrence are about 200 feet apart.

As portrayed in Hall's ***Picturesque memorials***, 1834. This view shows Mawarden Court and the parish church of St Lawrence almost side by side.

The church (above) and Mawarden Court (below) are in fact little changed from Hall's time.

2. Dunn's House

Dunn's Farm Seeds, established in 1832, moved to Salisbury just after World War One, and had offices in Castle Street and warehouses in Guilder Lane; they also rented space in the Market House. They built their handsome new premises in Scamell's Road just before the war.

Long vacated by the turn of the new millennium (the company had ceased trading in Salisbury by the 1970s), the property had become an eyesore.

It has since been refurbished and will be available as office space.

3. Ayleswade Bridge

An unusual perspective on the bridge from the west is offered in this watercolour by Edwin Young, painted in the local blacksmith's garden.

The modern view from the same spot.

4. Harnham Mill

As portrayed in Hall's ***Picturesque memorials***, 1834; originally in all probability a paper mill, in common with several others in the vicinity.

As it is today, a public house in a very picturesque spot.

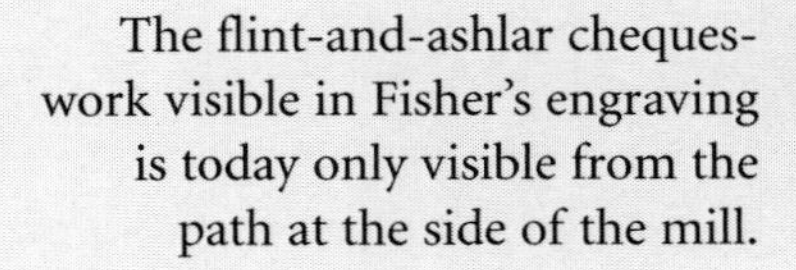

The flint-and-ashlar chequeswork visible in Fisher's engraving is today only visible from the path at the side of the mill.

FURTHER READING

Ayers, T. *Salisbury Cathedral: the West Front: a history and study in conservation* Phillimore, 2000

Ball, A.W. *Salisbury illustrated: the city's heritage in prints and drawings* Halsgrove, 2000

Bavin, J. *Heart of the city: the history of Salisbury Playhouse* pr. Salisbury Printing, 1976

Benson, R. and H. Hatcher *Old and New Sarum, or Salisbury* J.B. Nichols, 1843

Brimacombe, P. *A tale of two cathedrals: Old Sarum, New Salisbury* English Heritage, 1997

Britton, J. *The history and antiquities of the cathedral church of Salisbury* Longman, [etc.] for the author, 1814; repr. Paul Bush, 1999

Brown, S. *'Sumptuous and richly adorn'd': the decoration of Salisbury Cathedral* The Stationery Office [and the] Royal Commission on the Historical Monuments of England, 1999

Burnett, D. *Salisbury: the history of an English cathedral city* Compton Press, 1978

Chandler, J.H. *Endless Street: a history of Salisbury and its people* (Rev. ed.) Hobnob Press, 1987

— *Great-grandmother's footsteps: a stroll through Victorian Salisbury* Salisbury and South Wiltshire Museum, 1998

— *Salisbury: history and guide* Alan Sutton, 1992

— *Salisbury and its neighbours* Salisbury Civic Society, 1987

Cocke, T. and P. Kidson *Salisbury Cathedral: perspectives on the architectural history* HMSO [for the] Royal Commission on the Historical Monuments of England, 1993

Crittall, E. (Ed.) *A history of Wiltshire, vol. 6: the Borough of Wilton, the Borough of Old Salisbury, the City of New Salisbury, the Hundred of Underditch* Oxford University Press [for] the University of London Institute of Historical Research, 1962; repr. Dawson, 1984

Dictionary of National Biography – articles on Bowles, Britton, Hall, Hatcher, Wansey, etc.

Davies, J.S. (Ed.) *The Tropenell Cartulary. The Tropenell Cartulary, being the contents of an old Wiltshire muniment chest. Vol. 1.* Wiltshire Archaeological and Natural History Society, 1908.

Greenway, D. *Saint Osmund, Bishop of Salisbury, 1078-99: founder of the Cathedral at Old Sarum* RJL Smith and Associates for the Dean and Chapter of Salisbury Cathedral, 1999

Hall, P. *Picturesque memorials of Salisbury: a series of original etchings and vignettes ... of the most interesting buildings ... in that city and neighbourhood* W.B. Brodie, 1834

Haskins, C.H. *The ancient trade guilds and companies of Salisbury* Bennett, 1912

Hastings, A. *Elias of Dereham, architect of Salisbury Cathedral* RJL Smith and Associates for the Dean and Chapter of Salisbury Cathedral, 1997

MacLachlan, A. *The Civil War in Wiltshire* Rowan Books, 1997

Morriss, R.K. *The buildings of Salisbury; with photographs by Ken Hoverd* Alan Sutton, 1994

Mundy, F. and Co. *A directory of the city of Salisbury and surrounding districts* F. Mundy, 1891 (also subsequent directories, 1897–1925)

Newman, R. and J. Howells *Salisbury Past* Phillimore, 2001

Northy, T.J. *The popular history of Old and New Sarum* Wiltshire County Mirror and Express, 1897

Pope, W. *Life of Seth [Ward], Lord Bishop of Salisbury; ed. By J.B. Bamborough* Blackwell for the Luttrell Society, 1961

Price, F. *A series of particular and useful observations ... upon that admirable structure, the cathedral-church of Salisbury* C. and J. Ackers for R. Baldwin, 1753; repr. Salisbury and Stonehenge Editions, 1997

Rogers, K.H. and J.H. Chandler (Eds) *Early trade directories of Wiltshire, (1783–1842)* Wiltshire Record Society, 1992

Royal Commission on Historical Monuments (England) *Ancient and historical monuments in the city of Salisbury, vol. 1* HMSO, 1980

Salisbury Local History Group *Caring: a short history of Salisbury City Almshouse and other charities, from 14th to 20th centuries. 2nd ed.* Salisbury City Almshouse and Welfare Charities, 2000

Salisbury, South Wilts and Blackmore Museum *The festival book of Salisbury, published to commemorate the jubilee of the Museum 1864-1914; ed. F. Stevens* Bennett, 1914

Sharp, T. *Newer Sarum: a plan for Salisbury* Architectural Press for Salisbury City Council, 1949

Shemilt, P. *Salisbury 200: Salisbury Infirmary bicentenary review. 2nd ed.* Salisbury District Hospital League of Friends, 1992

Shortt, H. (Ed.) *City of Salisbury* Phoenix House, 1957; repr. S.R. Publishing, 1970

— *Salisbury: a new approach to the city and its neighbourhood* Longman, 1972

Slack, P. (Ed) *Poverty in early-Stuart Salisbury* Wiltshire Record Society, 1975 (Wiltshire Record Society Publications, vol. 31, for 1975)

Smith, G. *The Old Manor Hospital, Salisbury, Wiltshire: private madhouse, licensed house, psychiatric hospital*, 1979

Spring, R. *Salisbury Cathedral* (the new Bell's cathedral guides), Unwin Hyman, 1987

— *Salisbury Cathedral: a landmark in England's heritage* Dean and Chapter of Salisbury Cathedral, 1991

Tatton-Brown, T. *Great cathedrals of Britain* BBC Books, 1989

Temperley, H.W. and E. Brill *Ancient trackways of Wessex* Phoenix House, 1965

Turnbull, A. *The history of a city: Salisbury's first thousand years* *Salisbury Journal* in association with Salisbury District Council, 2001

Watkin, B. *A history of Wiltshire* (the Darwen county history series) Phillimore, 1989

Wroughton, J. *An unhappy Civil War: the experiences of ordinary people in Gloucestershire, Somerset and Wiltshire, 1642-1646* Lansdown Press, 1999

Illustration Credits

The author: 21, 22, 26, 42, 45, 46, 48, 65(x2), 80, 88, 91, 94, 97, 99(x2), 100, 107, 108(x2), 111(x2), 112, 113, 115, 116, 117(x2), 119, 121(x3), 122(x3), 123, 124(x3), 127(x2), 128(x3), 129(x4), 131, 132, 133, 134(x4), 135, 136, 137, 138, 139(x2), 140, 141(x2), 142(x2), 143(x3), 144, 145(x3), 146, 147(x3), 148, 149(x2), 151, 152(x2), 153, 154, 157(x2), 158(x2), 159(x3), 160, 161, 165, 166(x3), 168(x2); ***after* ACT information:** 120; **after Highways Agency information:** 94; ***after* James and Algar (*Wiltshire Archaeological and Natural History Magazine* 95(2002), p. 9):** 12; **by kind permission of the Vicar and Wardens of Grately St Leonard:** 36; **by kind permission of Hampshire County Council:** 33; **by kind permission of Sir Edward Heath:** 65; **by kind permission of the National Trust:** 64; **by kind permission of the Cure, Pontigny Abbey:** 29, 31; **by kind permission of Salisbury and South Wiltshire Museum:** 13, 16, 48, 67(x2), 82(x3); **by kind permission of Salisbury Cathedral:** 29, 30, 35(x2), 37, 38(x3), 64(x2), 74(x2), 75, 81, 104, 117, 161, 163(x3), 164; **by kind permission of Salisbury District Council:** 54, 65, 98; **by kind permission of Sarum Lacemakers:** 67; **by kind permission of the Rector and Wardens of Sarum St Thomas and St Edmund:** 47; **by kind permission of the Vicar and Wardens of Stratford-sub-Castle St Lawrence:** 166.

The Edwin Young Trust: 116(x2), 145, 148, 153, 167; **private collections (Mr David Brown):** 14, 142; **(the author):** 61; **Salisbury and South Wiltshire Museum:** 84, 105; **(Ephemera Collection):** 78 (x2), 83, 100; **(Photographic Collection):** 57, 143; **(Print Collection):** 60, 68, 69, 70, 71(x2), 85, 86, 109, 128, 130, 156; **(Sanger Collection):** 24, 90, 92, 109, 110, 127, 129, 139, 141, 142, 147(x2), 148(x2), 152, 158; **Salisbury Cathedral:** 32; **Salisbury District Council (Lovibond Collection):** 24, 53, 59, 90, 111, 128 (x2), 129, 132, 133, 134(x3), 135, 140(x2), 141(x3), 143, 144(x2), 146(x2), 147, 149, 154, 155, 159; **(Sharp, *Newer Sarum*):** 95, 96; **Salisbury Journal:** 148, 167.

Wiltshire County Council Libraries and Heritage: 25, 27, 40-1, 54, 58, 69(x2), 79, 81, 84, 87, 101(x2), 119, 135, 166; **(Benson and Hatcher, *Old and New Sarum*):** 34, 47, 72, 138; **(Britton, *Salisbury Cathedral*):**34, 35, 36, 162; **(Duke, *Prolusiones Historicae*):** 46; **(Ephemera Collection):** 114; **(Hall, *Picturesque Memorials*):** 2, 11, 26, 37, 43(x2), 45, 53, 55, 72(x2), 74, 97, 102, 103, 104, 139, 144, 145, 146, 150, 153, 157, 159, 160, 163(x2), 164, 165, 168; **Ordnance Survey Maps Sheets Wiltshire LXVI.11 and LXVI.7 (both 2nd ed., 1901):** 88, 165; **(Photographic Collection):** 73, 89, 91, 110, 114, 118, 123, 137, 147, 158(x2), 161; **(Price, *Observations*):** 28, 32, 33; **(Print Collection):** 17, 23, 24, 29, 41,42, 43, 50, 58, 59, 63, 74, 103, 108-9, 136, 150, 161; **(Richardson Collection):** 45, 106, 140; **(Gift of Mr Michael Rignal):** 113; **(Wiltshire and Swindon Record Office):** 49.

Index

New Street 9, 26, 65, 96, 106, 114, 144, 159, 164